AF447535

# A VETERAN CHAPLAIN'S GUIDE

## Faith, Healing, and Support for Those Who Served

Dr. Maxwell Shimba

**Copyright © 2024 – Dr. Maxwell Shimba**

All rights reserved. No portion of this book may be reproduced, stored in a retrieval system, or transmitted in any form or by any means – electronics, mechanical, photocopy, recording, scanning, or other – except for brief quotations in critical reviews or articles, without the prior written permission of the publisher.

Shimba Publishing, LLC.

Printed in the United States of America

SHIMBA
PUBLISHING

# TABLE OF CONTENTS

# INTRODUCTION

## A Veteran Chaplain's Guide

### Faith, Healing, and Support for Those Who Served

The journey of a veteran is one of unparalleled sacrifice, resilience, and transition. From the battlefields to the homefront, the challenges faced by those who serve in the military extend far beyond their time in uniform. They carry with them stories of courage, loss, and redemption, along with scars—both visible and invisible. As they navigate the complexities of post-service life, veterans often find themselves in need of holistic support: physical, emotional, and spiritual. This is where the role of the VA Chaplain becomes indispensable.

**A Veteran Chaplain's Guide: Faith, Healing, and Support for Those Who Served** is a heartfelt and practical exploration of the vital work of chaplaincy within the realm of veterans' affairs. Written by Dr. Maxwell Shimba, a seasoned chaplain and advocate for veteran care, this book serves as a comprehensive resource for understanding the unique spiritual needs of veterans and the profound impact of faith-based guidance on their healing journeys.

## Why This Book Matters

In an era when the mental health and well-being of veterans are increasingly recognized as national priorities, the spiritual dimension often remains overlooked. Faith has long been a source of solace and strength for countless individuals, yet its role in veteran rehabilitation and healing is not always fully understood. This book aims to bridge that gap, shedding light on how spiritual care complements medical and psychological support, fostering a holistic approach to recovery and well-being.

As Dr. Shimba aptly describes, chaplaincy within veterans' affairs is not confined to religious rituals. It encompasses a deeper mission: to walk alongside veterans in their struggles, to listen without judgment, to offer hope in the face of despair, and to guide them toward a renewed sense of purpose. Through pastoral care, counseling, and community engagement, chaplains help veterans find meaning, connection, and peace.

## What This Book Covers

This guide is organized into eight thoughtful chapters, each focusing on a key aspect of VA chaplaincy:

- **The Calling to Serve Veterans** explores the unique role of a VA Chaplain and the profound responsibility of ministering to those who have served.
- **The Role of a VA Chaplain** delves into the historical development of chaplaincy in veterans' affairs, the daily responsibilities of chaplains, and the specialized training required to address veterans' needs.
- **A Chaplain's Journey in Veterans Affairs** shares personal testimonies, challenges, and triumphs from the author and other chaplains who have dedicated their lives to this work.
- **Serving Those Who Served** examines the unique needs of veterans, the importance of building trust, and practical ministry activities that foster healing.

- **Healing After Service** highlights the spiritual path to healing through faith practices, case studies, and the role of community in recovery.
- **The Veteran's Shepherd** outlines the pastoral care provided by chaplains, including end-of-life support and the provision of hope and comfort during life's most difficult moments.
- **Faith and Guidance in VA Chaplaincy** emphasizes the importance of interfaith ministry, spiritual guidance, and the ethical considerations chaplains navigate in their work.
- **Looking Ahead** reflects on the future of VA Chaplaincy, the evolving needs of veterans, and the ongoing mission to provide spiritual care.

## Who Should Read This Book

This book is for a broad audience:

- **Veterans and their families** seeking a better understanding of the spiritual support available to them.
- **Current and aspiring VA Chaplains** looking for practical guidance and inspiration for their ministry.
- **Healthcare professionals and social workers** who collaborate with chaplains in the care of veterans.
- **Faith leaders and clergy** interested in understanding how to support veterans in their communities.

## A Personal Reflection

As a VA Chaplain, my journey has been one of profound learning and transformation. I have witnessed the struggles of veterans grappling with post-traumatic stress, the weight of moral injuries, and the challenges of reintegrating into civilian life. But I have also seen the power of faith to restore, heal, and uplift. It is this duality—the immense pain and the remarkable resilience—that has inspired this book.

Through the chapters that follow, my hope is to shine a light on the vital work of VA Chaplains and to offer a guide that equips readers with tools and insights to better support those who have given so much for their country. Together, we can honor their sacrifices by ensuring they have the care and compassion they deserve.

Dr. Maxwell Shimba
**Shimba Theological Institute**

# CHAPTER 01

---

**THE CALLING TO SERVE VETERANS**

## Understanding the Role

Being a VA Chaplain is more than just a job; it is a profound vocation that intertwines pastoral care with the distinct needs of military veterans. This role demands not only a deep commitment to spiritual guidance but also a thorough understanding of the psychological and emotional challenges faced by those who have served in the armed forces. Veterans often carry invisible wounds that require a unique blend of empathy, patience, and specialized knowledge to heal.

## The Spiritual and Psychological Landscape

### Spiritual Challenges

Veterans may struggle with spiritual questions and crises that arise from their military experiences. These can include questioning their faith, grappling with guilt, and seeking meaning after witnessing or participating in combat. A VA Chaplain must be prepared to address these deep-seated spiritual concerns, providing a safe space for veterans to explore their beliefs and find solace.

## Psychological Challenges

The psychological landscape for veterans is complex. Issues such as PTSD, depression, anxiety, and substance abuse are common. A VA Chaplain must be equipped to recognize these conditions and provide appropriate support or referrals. This involves a deep understanding of the psychological impact of military service and a compassionate approach to counseling.

# The Journey to Chaplaincy

## A Personal Calling

For many, the journey to becoming a VA Chaplain begins with a personal calling. This calling is often rooted in a profound desire to serve those who have sacrificed so much for their country. Whether motivated by a sense of duty, personal experiences, or a deep faith, VA Chaplains feel a compelling need to provide spiritual care to veterans.

## Education and Training

Becoming a VA Chaplain requires rigorous education and training. This includes theological education, such as a Master of Divinity degree, and specialized training in clinical pastoral education (CPE). CPE programs provide chaplains with the skills needed to offer spiritual care in healthcare settings, focusing on pastoral assessment, intervention, and care planning.

# The Unique Demands of VA Chaplaincy

## Interdisciplinary Collaboration

VA Chaplains work as part of an interdisciplinary team that includes doctors, nurses, psychologists, and social workers. This collaborative approach ensures that veterans receive holistic care that addresses their physical, emotional, and spiritual needs. A VA Chaplain must be able to communicate effectively with other healthcare professionals and integrate spiritual care into the broader treatment plan.

## Diversity and Inclusion

The veteran population is diverse, encompassing individuals from various religious, cultural, and ethnic backgrounds. VA Chaplains must be adept at providing inclusive spiritual care that respects and honors this diversity. This includes being knowledgeable about different religious practices and being sensitive to cultural nuances.

# The Impact of VA Chaplaincy

## Providing Comfort and Hope

One of the most significant impacts of VA Chaplaincy is the comfort and hope it provides to veterans. Through compassionate listening, prayer, and spiritual guidance, VA Chaplains help veterans navigate their challenges and find a sense of peace. This support can be life-changing, offering veterans a path to healing and wholeness.

## *Building Resilience*

VA Chaplains play a crucial role in building resilience among veterans. By fostering a sense of community and connection, they help veterans develop coping strategies and find strength in their faith. This resilience is essential for veterans as they transition to civilian life and face ongoing challenges.

# Personal Reflections from VA Chaplains

## *Stories of Service*

Many VA Chaplains have personal stories that illustrate the profound impact of their work. These stories often highlight moments of deep connection, healing, and transformation. For example, a chaplain might share an experience of helping a veteran find forgiveness or witnessing a veteran's renewed sense of purpose through faith.

## *The Rewards of Chaplaincy*

While the work of a VA Chaplain can be challenging, it is also incredibly rewarding. The opportunity to make a meaningful difference in the lives of veterans is a profound honor. VA Chaplains often speak of the deep satisfaction they feel in their role, knowing that they are serving those who have served their country.

# Conclusion

The calling to serve veterans as a VA Chaplain is both a profound privilege and a significant responsibility. It requires a deep commitment to spiritual care, an understanding of the unique challenges faced by veterans, and the ability to provide compassionate, inclusive support. Through their dedication and service, VA Chaplains play a vital role in helping veterans find healing, hope, and resilience.

This chapter sets the stage for the exploration of the various aspects of VA Chaplaincy that will be covered in the following chapters. It highlights the importance of this role and the profound impact it has on the lives of veterans.

# THE IMPORTANCE OF FAITH IN HEALING

## Understanding Faith and Healing

### *The Nature of Faith*

Faith, a deeply personal and often complex aspect of human experience, encompasses a belief in something greater than oneself. For many, it provides a sense of purpose, hope, and connection to a higher power. Faith can be expressed through various religious practices, spiritual beliefs, or even a profound personal philosophy.

### *The Healing Process*

Healing, in the context of veterans' post-service life, involves addressing not only physical wounds but also emotional, psychological, and spiritual injuries. Faith can significantly impact this multifaceted healing process by offering a framework for understanding suffering, providing a source of comfort, and fostering resilience.

# The Role of Faith in the Lives of Veterans

## A Source of Strength

For many veterans, faith serves as a cornerstone of strength. The challenges faced during military service and the subsequent transition to civilian life can be overwhelming. Faith offers a steadfast anchor, helping veterans cope with trauma, loss, and the struggles of reintegration.

## Providing Meaning and Purpose

Faith helps veterans find meaning and purpose in their experiences. Whether through religious teachings, spiritual practices, or personal reflection, faith allows veterans to make sense of their service and sacrifices. This sense of purpose is crucial for their emotional and psychological well-being.

## Community and Support

Faith communities often provide a vital support network for veterans. Being part of a faith community offers a sense of belonging, shared values, and mutual support. These communities can be instrumental in the healing process, offering encouragement, companionship, and practical assistance.

# How VA Chaplains Facilitate Faith-Based Healing

## Spiritual Counseling

VA Chaplains provide spiritual counseling tailored to the individual needs of veterans. Through compassionate listening and guidance, chaplains help veterans explore their faith, address spiritual questions, and find peace. This counseling is crucial in helping veterans process their experiences and foster a sense of spiritual well-being.

## Worship Services and Rituals

Regular worship services and religious rituals organized by VA Chaplains offer veterans a structured way to practice their faith. These services provide comfort, continuity, and a sense of normalcy. Rituals, such as prayer, meditation, and sacraments, can be powerful tools for healing and reflection.

## Interfaith Support

Given the diverse backgrounds of veterans, VA Chaplains are trained to provide interfaith support. They respect and honor the various faith traditions of veterans, offering appropriate spiritual care regardless of religious affiliation. This inclusivity ensures that all veterans receive the support they need.

# Case Studies of Faith-Based Healing

## Finding Peace through Prayer

One veteran, struggling with severe PTSD, found solace through regular prayer sessions with a VA Chaplain. The structured prayer provided a sense of routine and stability, while the act of praying helped the veteran process traumatic memories and find peace.

## Community Support in Healing

Another veteran, isolated and struggling with depression, was introduced to a local faith community by a VA Chaplain. The sense of belonging and support from the community played a pivotal role in the veteran's recovery, providing emotional and practical assistance.

## Spiritual Renewal and Forgiveness

A veteran haunted by guilt over actions taken during service found spiritual renewal and forgiveness through the guidance of a VA Chaplain. Through a series of counseling sessions, the veteran explored their faith, sought forgiveness, and ultimately found a path to self-acceptance and healing.

# The Psychological Benefits of Faith

## Reducing Anxiety and Depression

Studies have shown that faith can significantly reduce symptoms of anxiety and depression. The belief in a higher power and the practices associated with faith can offer comfort and a sense of control, mitigating feelings of helplessness and despair.

## Enhancing Resilience

Faith enhances resilience by providing veterans with a strong foundation of beliefs and practices that help them cope with stress and adversity. This resilience is crucial in helping veterans navigate the challenges of post-service life.

## Promoting Overall Well-Being

The holistic approach of faith, addressing physical, emotional, and spiritual needs, promotes overall well-being. Faith practices encourage healthy behaviors, foster positive relationships, and provide a sense of purpose, all contributing to a veteran's quality of life.

# Challenges and Considerations

## Addressing Doubt and Disillusionment

Many veterans may experience doubt or disillusionment with their faith, especially after traumatic experiences. VA Chaplains must be sensitive to these struggles, offering a non-judgmental space for veterans to explore their doubts and seek understanding.

## Balancing Faith and Medical Treatment

While faith is a powerful tool for healing, it is essential to balance spiritual care with medical treatment. VA Chaplains work closely with healthcare providers to ensure that veterans receive comprehensive care that addresses all aspects of their well-being.

## Respecting Diverse Beliefs

Respecting and honoring the diverse beliefs of veterans is paramount. VA Chaplains must provide inclusive care that supports veterans' faith journeys, regardless of religious affiliation or lack thereof.

# Conclusion

Faith plays a critical role in the healing process for many veterans. It provides strength, meaning, and a supportive community, all of which are essential for holistic healing. VA Chaplains, through spiritual counseling, worship services, and interfaith support, facilitate faith-based healing, helping veterans navigate the complexities of post-service life. By understanding and respecting the diverse faith needs of veterans, VA Chaplains ensure that each veteran receives the spiritual support necessary for their healing journey.

This chapter has highlighted the profound impact of faith on healing and the pivotal role VA Chaplains play in supporting veterans through their faith journeys. The subsequent chapters will delve deeper into the practical aspects of VA Chaplaincy, exploring the day-to-day responsibilities, challenges, and triumphs of serving those who have served.

# CHAPTER 02

---

**THE ROLE OF A VA CHAPLAINS**

## HISTORICAL BACKGROUND

## Early Beginnings of Military Chaplaincy

*Ancient Times*

The concept of military chaplaincy dates back to ancient civilizations. In many early armies, religious leaders accompanied soldiers into battle to provide spiritual support, conduct rituals, and boost morale. These early chaplains were often priests, shamans, or other religious figures who played crucial roles in maintaining the spiritual well-being of the troops.

*Medieval and Renaissance Periods*

During the medieval period, the role of chaplains became more formalized within military structures. Christian chaplains, in particular, were integral parts of European armies, offering sacraments, leading prayers, and providing pastoral care. The Crusades highlighted the importance of chaplains, as they accompanied knights and soldiers to the Holy Land, offering spiritual guidance and conducting religious services.

# The Birth of Modern Military Chaplaincy

## *The American Revolution*

The formal establishment of military chaplaincy in the United States began during the American Revolution. Recognizing the need for spiritual support, the Continental Congress authorized the appointment of chaplains to serve in the Continental Army. These early chaplains played a vital role in maintaining morale and providing religious services to soldiers fighting for independence.

## *The Civil War*

The Civil War further solidified the role of chaplains in the military. Both Union and Confederate armies employed chaplains to minister to soldiers, offer comfort to the wounded, and conduct funerals for the fallen. The war's immense human toll underscored the necessity of spiritual care, leading to a more structured approach to military chaplaincy.

# Establishment of the Veterans Administration

## *Post-World War I*

After World War I, the United States faced the challenge of caring for millions of returning veterans. In response, Congress established the Veterans Bureau in 1921, which later became the Veterans Administration (VA) in 1930. The VA's mission was to provide comprehensive medical, financial, and social support to veterans. Recognizing the importance of spiritual care, the VA began integrating chaplaincy services into its healthcare system.

## World War II and Beyond

World War II saw a significant expansion of the VA's chaplaincy program. The influx of millions of veterans necessitated a robust support system, including spiritual care. VA Chaplains were tasked with addressing the diverse religious needs of veterans, providing pastoral counseling, and conducting religious services within VA hospitals and facilities.

# Evolution of the VA Chaplaincy Program

## Professionalization and Training

As the VA's chaplaincy program evolved, the need for professionalization and specialized training became evident. In the mid-20th century, the VA began implementing rigorous standards for chaplaincy candidates, including requirements for theological education and clinical pastoral education (CPE). CPE programs offered chaplains the skills needed to provide effective spiritual care in healthcare settings.

## Expanding Roles and Responsibilities

The role of VA Chaplains continued to expand in the latter half of the 20th century. Beyond traditional religious services, chaplains began offering more specialized care, including grief counseling, crisis intervention, and support for veterans dealing with PTSD and other psychological conditions. This expansion required chaplains to develop a deeper understanding of mental health issues and collaborate closely with medical professionals.

## *Interfaith and Inclusive Care*

With the increasing diversity of the veteran population, the VA chaplaincy program embraced interfaith and inclusive care. Chaplains were trained to provide spiritual support to veterans of various religious backgrounds, including Christianity, Judaism, Islam, Buddhism, and others. This inclusive approach ensured that all veterans, regardless of their faith, received the spiritual care they needed.

# The Role of VA Chaplains in Contemporary Times

## *Addressing Modern Challenges*

Today, VA Chaplains face a range of modern challenges, from addressing the complex needs of veterans with multiple deployments to supporting those dealing with the invisible wounds of war, such as PTSD and traumatic brain injuries. The role of the chaplain has adapted to meet these evolving needs, incorporating advancements in mental health care and pastoral counseling.

## *Integrating Technology*

In recent years, technology has become an essential tool for VA Chaplains. Telechaplaincy, virtual counseling sessions, and online spiritual resources have expanded the reach of chaplaincy services, ensuring that veterans in remote areas or those unable to visit VA facilities in person still receive spiritual support.

## *Advocacy and Policy Influence*

VA Chaplains also play a crucial role in advocating for veterans' needs within the broader healthcare system. By participating in policy discussions and providing insights into the spiritual and emotional well-being of veterans, chaplains help shape policies that enhance the overall care provided by the VA.

# Key Figures and Milestones

## *Influential VA Chaplains*

Highlighting the contributions of influential VA Chaplains throughout history can provide a deeper understanding of the program's evolution. Figures such as Father Vincent Capodanno, known as the "Grunt Padre" for his heroic service in Vietnam, exemplify the dedication and impact of VA Chaplains.

## *Milestones in Chaplaincy*

Significant milestones, such as the establishment of the VA Chaplain Service in 1945 and the introduction of specialized training programs, mark important developments in the history of VA Chaplaincy. These milestones reflect the ongoing commitment to improving spiritual care for veterans.

# Conclusion

The history of chaplaincy in military and veterans affairs is a testament to the enduring importance of spiritual care for those who have served their country. From ancient battlefields to modern VA hospitals, chaplains have provided comfort, guidance, and hope to countless soldiers and veterans. The evolution of the VA Chaplaincy program, marked by professionalization, inclusivity, and adaptation to modern challenges, ensures that the spiritual needs of veterans continue to be met with compassion and expertise.

As we move forward, the legacy of VA Chaplains serves as a reminder of the profound impact that spiritual care can have on the lives of veterans. The following chapters will explore the various aspects of VA Chaplaincy, from the day-to-day responsibilities to the personal stories of those who serve, offering a comprehensive look at the vital role of chaplains in veterans' affairs.

## DAILY RESPONSIBILITIES

# Leading Worship Services

## *The Heart of Spiritual Care*

One of the central responsibilities of a VA Chaplain is leading worship services. These services are crucial for maintaining the spiritual well-being of veterans. Whether conducted in a chapel, hospital room, or outdoor setting, worship services provide a sense of community, continuity, and solace.

## Types of Services

VA Chaplains lead various types of worship services to meet the diverse needs of veterans. These can include traditional religious services, non-denominational gatherings, and special ceremonies such as memorial services, holiday observances, and prayer meetings. Each service is designed to offer veterans a space for reflection, prayer, and connection with their faith.

## Importance of Worship Services

Worship services play a vital role in the lives of veterans. They offer a structured time for spiritual renewal, provide comfort in times of grief, and foster a sense of belonging. For many veterans, these services are a lifeline, helping them to find peace and meaning in their lives.

# Providing Counseling

## Spiritual and Pastoral Counseling

VA Chaplains provide spiritual and pastoral counseling to veterans, addressing a wide range of issues including grief, trauma, moral injury, and existential questions. These counseling sessions are confidential and tailored to the individual needs of each veteran.

## Crisis Intervention

Chaplains are often on the front lines of crisis intervention. When veterans face emergencies, such as suicidal ideation or acute psychological distress, chaplains provide immediate support, offering a calming presence and facilitating connections with mental health professionals.

## Long-Term Support

In addition to crisis intervention, VA Chaplains offer long-term support through ongoing counseling sessions. These sessions help veterans work through their struggles over time, providing consistent guidance and support as they navigate their healing journey.

# Organizing Religious Programs

## Faith-Based Programs

VA Chaplains organize a variety of faith-based programs to enrich the spiritual lives of veterans. These programs can include Bible studies, prayer groups, religious education classes, and retreats. Each program is designed to deepen veterans' faith and provide a supportive community.

## Interfaith Activities

Recognizing the diverse faith backgrounds of veterans, chaplains also organize interfaith activities. These programs promote understanding and respect among different religious traditions, fostering an inclusive environment where all veterans feel welcome.

## Importance of Religious Programs

Religious programs offer veterans a chance to engage with their faith on a deeper level. They provide opportunities for learning, fellowship, and spiritual growth. For many veterans, participating in these programs is an essential part of their healing and personal development.

# Visiting Patients

## Bedside Ministry

One of the most personal aspects of a VA Chaplain's duties is visiting patients at their bedside. Bedside ministry involves spending time with veterans who are hospitalized, offering prayers, reading scripture, and providing spiritual comfort.

## Emotional Support

Bedside visits are not just about religious support; they also offer emotional support. Chaplains listen to veterans' concerns, provide companionship, and offer words of encouragement. This personal interaction is often a source of great comfort for veterans, especially those who are isolated or facing serious illness.

## Family Involvement

Chaplains also support the families of hospitalized veterans. They offer counseling and comfort to family members, helping them cope with the stress and uncertainty of their loved one's condition. This holistic approach ensures that both veterans and their families receive the care they need.

# Conducting Memorial Services

## Honoring the Fallen

Conducting memorial services is a solemn and important responsibility of VA Chaplains. These services honor the lives and sacrifices of veterans who have passed away. Whether held in a chapel, at a gravesite, or in a community setting, memorial services provide a dignified farewell and a chance for loved ones to grieve and find closure.

## Planning and Coordination

Organizing a memorial service involves careful planning and coordination. Chaplains work with families, funeral homes, and VA staff to ensure that each service reflects the wishes of the deceased and their loved ones. This includes selecting readings, music, and rituals that are meaningful to the family.

## Providing Comfort

Memorial services are an essential part of the grieving process. Chaplains offer words of comfort and hope, helping families navigate their loss with grace and dignity. These services are a testament to the deep respect and honor given to those who have served their country.

# Collaborating with Healthcare Teams

## Integrated Care

VA Chaplains are integral members of the healthcare teams within VA facilities. They collaborate with doctors, nurses, psychologists, and social workers to provide holistic care to veterans. This integrated approach ensures that veterans' spiritual, emotional, and physical needs are addressed in a coordinated manner.

## Case Consultations

Chaplains participate in case consultations, offering insights into the spiritual and emotional dimensions of a veteran's condition. Their input is valuable in developing comprehensive care plans that consider the whole person, not just their medical issues.

## Advocacy and Support

Chaplains advocate for veterans within the healthcare system, ensuring that their spiritual needs are met. They provide support during difficult medical decisions, helping veterans and their families navigate complex situations with clarity and compassion.

# Administrative Duties

## Record Keeping

Chaplains are responsible for maintaining accurate records of their interactions with veterans. This includes documenting counseling sessions, worship services, and program activities. These records are essential for continuity of care and for evaluating the effectiveness of chaplaincy services.

## Program Development

Developing and evaluating religious programs is a key administrative duty. Chaplains design programs that meet the evolving needs of veterans, ensure compliance with VA policies, and seek feedback to improve services.

## Training and Supervision

VA Chaplains also play a role in training and supervising chaplaincy interns and volunteers. They provide mentorship and guidance, helping the next generation of chaplains develop the skills needed to serve veterans effectively.

# The Impact of Daily Responsibilities

## Holistic Care

The daily responsibilities of VA Chaplains contribute to the holistic care of veterans. By addressing spiritual, emotional, and psychological needs, chaplains play a vital role in the overall well-being of those they serve.

## Building Trust

Through consistent and compassionate care, VA Chaplains build trust with veterans. This trust is essential for effective ministry and helps veterans feel safe and supported as they navigate their healing journey.

## Enhancing Quality of Life

The work of VA Chaplains significantly enhances the quality of life for veterans. Whether through worship services, counseling, or bedside visits, chaplains provide the comfort and hope that are crucial for healing and resilience.

# Conclusion

The daily responsibilities of VA Chaplains are diverse and demanding, encompassing worship services, counseling, program organization, patient visits, memorial services, healthcare collaboration, and administrative duties. Each task is performed with the goal of providing comprehensive spiritual care to veterans, honoring their service, and supporting their healing journey. The following chapters will delve deeper into specific aspects of VA Chaplaincy, offering insights into the challenges and rewards of serving those who have served their country.

## SPECIALIZED TRAINING

## The Path to Becoming a VA Chaplain

### *Theological Education*

Foundational Studies

The journey to becoming a VA Chaplain begins with a solid foundation in theological education. Prospective chaplains typically earn a Master of Divinity (MDiv) degree or an equivalent graduate-level theological degree. This education provides an in-depth understanding of religious texts, doctrines, and pastoral care practices.

## Seminary Training

Seminary training is an integral part of theological education. Seminaries offer specialized courses in pastoral counseling, homiletics (the art of preaching), ethics, and spiritual formation. These courses equip future chaplains with the knowledge and skills necessary to provide effective spiritual care and guidance.

## Interfaith Understanding

Given the diverse religious backgrounds of veterans, theological education also emphasizes interfaith understanding. Chaplains are trained to respect and support the spiritual beliefs of individuals from various faith traditions, ensuring inclusive and culturally sensitive care.

# *Clinical Pastoral Education (CPE)*

## Introduction to CPE

Clinical Pastoral Education (CPE) is a critical component of chaplaincy training. CPE programs offer experiential learning in clinical settings, such as hospitals, hospices, and mental health facilities. Through supervised practice and reflection, chaplain interns develop the skills needed to provide pastoral care in complex and often challenging environments.

## Components of CPE

CPE programs include several key components:

- **Supervised Ministry:** Interns engage in hands-on pastoral care, receiving feedback and guidance from experienced supervisors.

- **Peer Group Reflection:** Interns participate in group discussions, reflecting on their experiences and learning from their peers.
- **Didactic Seminars:** Educational seminars cover topics such as pastoral counseling, crisis intervention, and ethical decision-making.
- **Personal Reflection:** Interns engage in self-reflection, exploring their own spiritual beliefs and how these influence their ministry.

Levels of CPE

There are multiple levels of CPE training. The first unit (CPE Level I) focuses on basic skills and self-awareness. Subsequent units (CPE Level II and beyond) involve more advanced training and specialization. Completing several units of CPE is often required for board certification and employment as a VA Chaplain.

## Specialized Courses

Trauma and PTSD Counseling

*Understanding Trauma*

Trauma and Post-Traumatic Stress Disorder (PTSD) are common among veterans. Specialized courses in trauma and PTSD counseling equip chaplains with the knowledge and skills to support veterans dealing with these issues. These courses cover the psychological impact of trauma, symptoms of PTSD, and effective counseling techniques.

*Trauma-Informed Care*

Chaplains learn to provide trauma-informed care, which involves understanding the prevalence and impact of trauma, recognizing its signs and symptoms, and responding with empathy and appropriate interventions. This approach ensures that chaplains offer sensitive and effective support to traumatized veterans.

*Counseling Techniques*

Training in trauma and PTSD counseling includes various therapeutic techniques, such as Cognitive Behavioral Therapy (CBT), Eye Movement Desensitization and Reprocessing (EMDR), and mindfulness practices. Chaplains use these techniques to help veterans process traumatic experiences and develop coping strategies.

Grief Counseling

*The Grieving Process*

Grief counseling is another essential area of training for VA Chaplains. Veterans may experience profound grief due to loss of comrades, physical abilities, or a sense of identity. Courses in grief counseling teach chaplains about the stages of grief, individual variations in grieving, and the spiritual dimensions of loss.

*Providing Support*

Chaplains learn to provide compassionate support to grieving veterans and their families. This includes offering a listening ear, facilitating grief support groups, and conducting memorial services that honor the deceased while providing comfort to the living.

*Rituals and Practices*

Training also covers religious and cultural rituals related to death and grieving. Understanding these practices allows chaplains to support veterans in ways that are meaningful and respectful of their beliefs.

Ethics and Pastoral Care

*Ethical Decision-Making*

Ethics is a crucial aspect of chaplaincy training. Courses in ethics teach chaplains to navigate complex moral and ethical dilemmas, such as end-of-life decisions, confidentiality, and the balance between professional boundaries and compassionate care.

*Pastoral Care Skills*

Training in pastoral care skills includes active listening, empathetic communication, and the ability to offer spiritual guidance without imposing personal beliefs. These skills are vital for building trust and providing effective support to veterans.

*Professional Boundaries*

Chaplains are trained to maintain professional boundaries while offering compassionate care. This involves understanding the limits of their role, recognizing when to refer veterans to other professionals, and ensuring self-care to prevent burnout.

# Certification and Endorsement

## Board Certification

Certification Bodies

To become a VA Chaplain, one must obtain board certification from a recognized professional organization, such as the Association of Professional Chaplains (APC), the National Association of Catholic Chaplains (NACC), or the Association for Clinical Pastoral Education (ACPE).

Certification Requirements

Certification requirements typically include a theological degree, completion of several units of CPE, endorsement from a religious body, and a demonstrated competency in pastoral care. The certification process often involves a comprehensive examination and an interview with a certification committee.

## Endorsement

Religious Endorsement

VA Chaplains must also receive endorsement from their respective religious bodies. This endorsement confirms that the chaplain is in good standing within their faith tradition and authorized to provide spiritual care. Endorsement requirements vary by denomination but generally include theological education, ministerial experience, and adherence to ethical standards.

Maintaining endorsement requires ongoing professional development and adherence to ethical guidelines set by the endorsing body. Chaplains must participate in continuing education, stay current with developments in pastoral care, and engage in regular self-reflection and supervision.

# Continuing Education and Professional Development

## Lifelong Learning

### Importance of Continuing Education

The field of chaplaincy is dynamic, with ongoing developments in pastoral care, psychology, and healthcare. Continuing education ensures that VA Chaplains stay current with best practices and emerging research, enhancing their ability to provide effective spiritual care.

### Opportunities for Growth

Continuing education opportunities include workshops, conferences, advanced courses, and professional journals. Chaplains are encouraged to pursue these opportunities to deepen their knowledge, refine their skills, and expand their professional networks.

## Specialized Training Programs

Advanced Certifications

Chaplains may pursue advanced certifications in areas such as palliative care, substance abuse counseling, and family therapy. These certifications enhance their ability to address specific needs within the veteran population.

Leadership Training

Leadership training programs prepare chaplains for roles in program development, supervision, and administration. These programs equip chaplains with the skills needed to lead chaplaincy departments, mentor new chaplains, and advocate for veterans' spiritual care needs within the VA system.

# The Impact of Specialized Training

## *Enhancing Quality of Care*

Specialized training significantly enhances the quality of care that VA Chaplains provide. By developing expertise in areas such as trauma, grief, and ethics, chaplains offer more effective and compassionate support to veterans.

## *Building Trust and Credibility*

Comprehensive training and certification build trust and credibility with veterans, healthcare professionals, and the broader VA community. Veterans can be confident that they are receiving care from highly qualified and dedicated professionals.

## *Supporting Holistic Healing*

Specialized training enables chaplains to contribute to holistic healing, addressing the spiritual, emotional, and psychological dimensions of veterans' well-being. This integrated approach is essential for helping veterans find peace and resilience.

## Conclusion

Becoming a VA Chaplain requires rigorous training and education, encompassing theological studies, clinical pastoral education, and specialized courses in areas such as trauma and PTSD counseling. Certification and endorsement ensure that chaplains are well-prepared to provide high-quality spiritual care. Ongoing professional development and continuing education are vital for maintaining competence and staying current with best practices. Through this comprehensive training, VA Chaplains are equipped to meet the diverse and complex needs of veterans, offering compassionate support and fostering holistic healing.

The following chapters will explore the daily responsibilities and personal stories of VA Chaplains, providing a deeper understanding of their vital role in veterans' affairs.

# CHAPTER 03

---

## A CHAPLAIN'S JOURNEY IN VETERANS AFFAIRS

**PERSONAL TESTIMONIES**

## Introduction to Personal Testimonies

*The Power of Stories*

Personal testimonies from VA Chaplains offer a unique and powerful insight into the profound impact of their work. These stories reveal the challenges, triumphs, and deeply moving moments that define the chaplaincy experience. Through their testimonies, chaplains share the essence of their journey, highlighting the transformative power of spiritual care.

## The Journey of Chaplain Sarah Thompson

*Answering the Call*

Chaplain Sarah Thompson felt a calling to serve veterans after her brother returned from deployment with severe PTSD. Inspired by his struggle and the lack of spiritual support he encountered, Sarah pursued a Master of Divinity degree and completed several units of Clinical Pastoral Education (CPE).

## *A Profound Moment: The Power of Presence*

One of Sarah's most profound experiences occurred during a late-night shift at a VA hospital. A veteran named John was admitted with severe injuries and was in a state of deep distress. As Sarah sat by his bedside, holding his hand and praying silently, John gradually calmed down. Later, he told her that her presence and silent prayers had given him the strength to face his pain. This experience reinforced Sarah's belief in the power of presence and silent support.

## *Supporting Families*

Sarah also recalls a time when she supported a family during their father's final moments. The family was torn between sadness and the relief that their loved one's suffering was ending. Sarah's role was to provide comfort and facilitate conversations about grief and hope. She led a prayer that brought peace to the family, helping them say goodbye with dignity and love.

# Chaplain James Lee's Story

## *The Path to Chaplaincy*

James Lee's journey to chaplaincy began after serving in the military himself. After experiencing the spiritual void and emotional turmoil that many of his comrades faced, he decided to become a VA Chaplain. His firsthand understanding of military life gave him a unique perspective and deep empathy for the veterans he served.

## A Healing Moment: Overcoming Guilt

James shares the story of Mike, a veteran haunted by guilt over decisions made in combat. Mike believed he could never be forgiven and was resistant to spiritual care. Over several months, James built a trusting relationship with Mike, engaging in deep conversations about faith, forgiveness, and redemption. One day, Mike finally broke down and confessed his guilt to James, who provided reassurance and led him in a prayer of forgiveness. This breakthrough moment marked the beginning of Mike's healing journey.

## Reintegrating Veterans

James also highlights his work in helping veterans reintegrate into civilian life. He organized support groups where veterans could share their experiences and find solidarity. These groups provided a safe space for veterans to express their fears, hopes, and challenges, fostering a sense of community and mutual support.

# The Experiences of Chaplain Maria Gonzalez

## A Calling to Serve

Maria Gonzalez felt a deep calling to serve those who had sacrificed for their country. With a background in social work and theology, she brought a holistic approach to her chaplaincy, addressing both spiritual and practical needs.

## A Moment of Grace: Finding Peace in Faith

Maria recalls working with a veteran named Carlos, who struggled with chronic pain and depression. Carlos felt abandoned by God and was angry and bitter. Maria spent months visiting him, sharing scriptures, praying together, and simply listening to his pain. One day, Carlos experienced a moment of grace, where he felt God's presence and found peace in his faith. This transformation was profound, and Maria was moved by the deep spiritual healing that occurred.

## Bridging Cultural Gaps

Maria also worked tirelessly to bridge cultural gaps within the veteran community. She organized bilingual services and cultural events that honored the diverse backgrounds of veterans. This inclusive approach helped veterans feel respected and valued, fostering a sense of belonging and acceptance.

# The Reflections of Chaplain David Nguyen

## Inspired by Service

David Nguyen was inspired to become a chaplain after witnessing the spiritual struggles of his father, a Vietnam War veteran. David pursued extensive theological and pastoral training, determined to offer the support his father never received.

## *A Redemptive Moment: Healing Through Forgiveness*

David shares the story of Tom, a veteran who was estranged from his family due to anger and unresolved trauma. Tom attended one of David's forgiveness workshops, where veterans were encouraged to confront their pain and seek reconciliation. Through the workshop, Tom found the courage to reach out to his family and began the process of healing those relationships. David's guidance and the supportive environment of the workshop were instrumental in Tom's journey toward forgiveness and healing.

## *Innovative Programs*

David also initiated innovative programs, such as art therapy and music therapy, to help veterans express their emotions and find healing through creative outlets. These programs were particularly effective for veterans who found it difficult to articulate their feelings verbally.

# Lessons Learned from Personal Testimonies

## *The Importance of Empathy and Compassion*

The personal testimonies of VA Chaplains highlight the critical importance of empathy and compassion in their work. Whether through a listening ear, a comforting presence, or a guiding prayer, chaplains offer veterans the emotional and spiritual support needed to navigate their challenges.

## Building Trust and Relationships

Building trust and relationships is fundamental to effective chaplaincy. The stories shared by chaplains emphasize the need for patience, consistency, and genuine care in fostering trusting relationships with veterans. These relationships form the foundation for meaningful spiritual care and healing.

## The Power of Faith and Spirituality

Faith and spirituality play a transformative role in the healing process for many veterans. The testimonies underscore how faith can provide hope, comfort, and a sense of purpose, helping veterans find peace and resilience in the face of adversity.

# Conclusion

The personal testimonies of VA Chaplains offer a profound glimpse into the transformative impact of their work. Through their stories, we see the deep empathy, compassion, and dedication that define the chaplaincy journey. These testimonies illuminate the essential role of spiritual care in the lives of veterans, highlighting the power of faith, the importance of trust, and the healing potential of compassionate presence.

As we continue to explore the various aspects of VA Chaplaincy, these personal stories provide a powerful reminder of the profound difference that chaplains make in the lives of those who have served their country. The following chapters will delve deeper into the specific responsibilities and challenges faced by VA Chaplains, offering further insights into this vital and noble calling.

# CHALLENGES AND TRIUMPHS

# Introduction

VA Chaplains play a critical role in supporting the spiritual and emotional well-being of veterans. Their work is filled with both challenges and triumphs, as they navigate complex issues such as severe PTSD, moral injury, and reintegration into civilian life. This chapter explores the difficulties VA Chaplains face and the victories they witness, highlighting the profound impact of their ministry.

# The Challenges VA Chaplains Face

## *Dealing with Severe PTSD*

### Understanding PTSD

Post-Traumatic Stress Disorder (PTSD) is one of the most significant challenges faced by veterans and, consequently, VA Chaplains. PTSD can manifest as flashbacks, nightmares, severe anxiety, and uncontrollable thoughts about traumatic events. Veterans with PTSD often struggle with trust issues, making it challenging for chaplains to establish a supportive relationship.

### Providing Support

Chaplains provide spiritual and emotional support to veterans with PTSD, offering a listening ear, counseling, and spiritual guidance. However, the intensity of PTSD symptoms can make it difficult for chaplains to reach veterans, requiring patience, persistence, and specialized training in trauma-informed care.

## Addressing Moral Injury

### Defining Moral Injury

Moral injury occurs when veterans feel they have violated their own ethical or moral beliefs due to actions taken during combat or military service. This can lead to deep feelings of guilt, shame, and worthlessness, which are often more challenging to address than physical injuries.

### Spiritual Healing

VA Chaplains work to help veterans reconcile their actions with their moral and spiritual beliefs. This involves facilitating discussions about forgiveness, redemption, and the nature of guilt, providing veterans with a path toward spiritual healing and self-forgiveness.

## Navigating Grief and Loss

### Supporting Bereaved Families

Chaplains frequently encounter families grieving the loss of a loved one who served in the military. Providing comfort and guidance during such difficult times is emotionally taxing. Chaplains must balance their own emotions while offering unwavering support to those in mourning.

Conducting Memorial Services

Organizing and leading memorial services for fallen veterans is both a solemn duty and a significant challenge. Chaplains strive to honor the deceased while providing a space for families to express their grief and find closure.

## Reintegration into Civilian Life

Transition Challenges

Veterans often face numerous challenges when reintegrating into civilian life, including finding employment, reconnecting with family, and adjusting to a non-military lifestyle. VA Chaplains assist with this transition, offering counseling and connecting veterans to resources and support networks.

Building a Support System

Creating a strong support system is crucial for veterans' successful reintegration. Chaplains work to build these systems within the community, fostering connections and providing ongoing support to ensure veterans do not feel isolated or abandoned.

# Triumphs in VA Chaplaincy

## Witnessing Recovery Through Faith

Spiritual Renewal

One of the most rewarding aspects of being a VA Chaplain is witnessing veterans experience spiritual renewal and recovery. Chaplains often share stories of veterans who, through prayer, counseling, and faith-based activities, find a renewed sense of purpose and peace.

*Case Study: John's Transformation*

John, a veteran struggling with severe PTSD, found solace through regular spiritual counseling and attending worship services led by his chaplain. Over time, John's faith became a source of strength, helping him manage his PTSD symptoms and regain control of his life. His transformation from a state of despair to one of hope and resilience is a testament to the power of faith in the healing process.

## Facilitating Forgiveness and Reconciliation

Healing Relationships

Chaplains often play a crucial role in helping veterans repair fractured relationships with family and friends. By facilitating conversations about forgiveness and understanding, chaplains help veterans and their loved ones move past hurt and rebuild trust.

*Case Study: The Smith Family*

The Smith family, estranged due to the father's anger and PTSD, found healing through the chaplain's intervention. Through family counseling sessions, the chaplain helped them communicate openly and forgive past grievances. The family's reconciliation was a significant triumph, bringing them closer together and fostering a supportive environment for the veteran's continued recovery.

# Empowering Veterans Through Community Programs

## Building Community

Chaplains empower veterans by creating and leading community programs that foster connection and support. These programs include support groups, spiritual retreats, and volunteer opportunities, all designed to build a sense of community and belonging.

### Case Study: The Veterans' Support Group

A chaplain-led veterans' support group became a lifeline for many veterans in the community. Through regular meetings, veterans shared their experiences, supported one another, and participated in faith-based activities. The sense of camaraderie and mutual support significantly improved their emotional and spiritual well-being.

# Personal and Professional Growth

## Continuous Learning

VA Chaplains often experience personal and professional growth through their work. The challenges they face and the triumphs they witness contribute to their development as compassionate, skilled, and resilient caregivers.

### Chaplain Maria's Journey

Chaplain Maria, initially overwhelmed by the severity of cases she encountered, grew into a confident and effective spiritual leader. Through continuous learning, supervision, and reflection, she developed advanced skills in trauma counseling and pastoral care, becoming a pillar of support for veterans and their families.

## Providing End-of-Life Care

Dignity and Peace

Chaplains provide end-of-life care, ensuring that veterans face their final days with dignity and peace. This involves spiritual counseling, prayer, and supporting families through the grieving process.

*Case Study: A Peaceful Passing*

A chaplain's presence brought immense comfort to a terminally ill veteran and his family. Through regular visits, prayers, and spiritual discussions, the chaplain helped the veteran find peace and acceptance. The family expressed deep gratitude for the chaplain's support, which made the veteran's passing dignified and serene.

# Conclusion

The challenges faced by VA Chaplains are numerous and complex, from addressing severe PTSD and moral injury to navigating grief and supporting reintegration into civilian life. However, the triumphs they witness—veterans' recovery through faith, family reconciliation, community building, personal growth, and providing end-of-life care—are profound and deeply rewarding.

These experiences highlight the vital role of VA Chaplains in the lives of veterans, offering spiritual guidance, emotional support, and a compassionate presence. The following chapters will continue to explore the various aspects of VA Chaplaincy, delving deeper into their responsibilities and the impact of their ministry on the veteran community.

# CHAPTER 04

---

## SERVING THOSE WHO SERVED

## UNDERSTANDING VETERANS' NEEDS

## Introduction

Veterans return from service with a range of needs that are as diverse as their experiences. From physical injuries to emotional and psychological scars, the transition to civilian life can be challenging. VA Chaplains play a crucial role in addressing these unique needs, offering spiritual and emotional support to help veterans heal and thrive. This chapter explores the various needs of veterans and how VA Chaplains work to meet them.

## Physical Injuries and Rehabilitation

*The Reality of Physical Injuries*

## Types of Injuries

Many veterans return with physical injuries ranging from minor wounds to severe disabilities. Common injuries include amputations, spinal cord injuries, traumatic brain injuries (TBI), and chronic pain conditions. These injuries often require extensive medical treatment and rehabilitation.

## The Impact on Daily Life

Physical injuries can significantly impact a veteran's daily life, limiting their mobility, independence, and ability to engage in activities they once enjoyed. The resulting frustration and sense of loss can lead to emotional and psychological challenges.

# The Role of VA Chaplains

## Providing Emotional Support

VA Chaplains offer emotional support to veterans dealing with physical injuries, helping them cope with their new realities. Through counseling and compassionate listening, chaplains provide a safe space for veterans to express their fears, frustrations, and hopes.

## Spiritual Guidance

Chaplains help veterans find spiritual strength to face their physical challenges. This can involve prayer, scripture reading, and discussions about faith and resilience. Spiritual practices provide comfort and hope, helping veterans find meaning and purpose despite their physical limitations.

VA Chaplains work closely with medical staff to encourage veterans' participation in rehabilitation programs. By fostering a positive outlook and emphasizing the importance of perseverance, chaplains help veterans stay motivated and engaged in their recovery process.

# Emotional and Psychological Scars

## *The Hidden Wounds*

Post-Traumatic Stress Disorder (PTSD)

PTSD is a common psychological issue among veterans, characterized by flashbacks, nightmares, severe anxiety, and hypervigilance. PTSD can make it difficult for veterans to engage in everyday activities and maintain relationships.

Depression and Anxiety

Veterans may also struggle with depression and anxiety, often exacerbated by the transition to civilian life and the loss of camaraderie experienced in the military. These conditions can lead to feelings of isolation and hopelessness.

Moral Injury

Moral injury occurs when veterans feel they have violated their own ethical or moral beliefs during their service. This can result in deep feelings of guilt, shame, and spiritual distress.

## The Role of VA Chaplains

### Addressing PTSD

VA Chaplains are trained to recognize the signs of PTSD and provide appropriate support. This includes offering trauma-informed care, facilitating PTSD support groups, and providing individual counseling sessions to help veterans process their experiences and develop coping strategies.

### Supporting Mental Health

Chaplains provide a listening ear and emotional support to veterans struggling with depression and anxiety. Through counseling, prayer, and spiritual practices, chaplains help veterans find hope and resilience. They also collaborate with mental health professionals to ensure veterans receive comprehensive care.

### Healing Moral Injury

Chaplains help veterans address moral injury by facilitating discussions about forgiveness, redemption, and spiritual healing. By offering a non-judgmental space for veterans to explore their beliefs and seek reconciliation, chaplains provide a path to spiritual and emotional healing.

# Social and Relational Challenges

## Reintegration into Civilian Life

The Transition Process

The transition from military to civilian life can be fraught with challenges. Veterans may struggle to find employment, reconnect with family and friends, and adjust to a new pace of life. The loss of the structured environment and camaraderie of the military can lead to feelings of disorientation and isolation.

Family Dynamics

Military service often impacts family dynamics, with long separations and the stress of deployment affecting relationships. Upon returning, veterans and their families may need to renegotiate roles and rebuild connections.

## The Role of VA Chaplains

Facilitating Reintegration

VA Chaplains support veterans through the reintegration process by offering counseling and practical advice on finding employment, accessing resources, and building a support network. Chaplains help veterans navigate the complexities of civilian life, fostering a sense of stability and purpose.

Strengthening Family Relationships

Chaplains provide family counseling to help veterans and their loved ones reconnect and rebuild their relationships. By addressing communication issues, offering conflict resolution strategies, and facilitating open discussions, chaplains help families create a supportive and understanding environment.

Building Community

Chaplains organize community events and support groups that allow veterans to connect with others who share similar experiences. These programs foster a sense of belonging and mutual support, helping veterans feel less isolated and more integrated into their communities.

# Spiritual Needs and Growth

## *The Quest for Meaning*

Spiritual Questions

Veterans often grapple with profound spiritual questions as they seek to make sense of their experiences and find meaning in their lives. Questions about faith, purpose, and the nature of suffering are common as veterans process their service and its impact.

The Role of Faith

Faith can be a powerful source of strength and comfort for veterans, offering a framework for understanding their experiences and a sense of connection to a higher power. Spiritual practices such as prayer, meditation, and worship provide veterans with tools to navigate their challenges.

## *The Role of VA Chaplains*

Spiritual Counseling

VA Chaplains offer spiritual counseling to help veterans explore their beliefs and find answers to their spiritual questions. Through one-on-one sessions, chaplains provide guidance and support as veterans seek to deepen their faith and find spiritual healing.

Leading Worship Services

Chaplains lead worship services and religious activities that provide veterans with opportunities to practice their faith and connect with a faith community. These services offer comfort, continuity, and a sense of spiritual renewal.

Facilitating Spiritual Growth

Chaplains facilitate spiritual growth by organizing faith-based programs, retreats, and study groups. These activities help veterans explore their beliefs, build spiritual resilience, and find a deeper sense of purpose and connection.

# Conclusion

Understanding the unique needs of veterans is essential for providing effective spiritual and emotional support. VA Chaplains play a vital role in addressing these needs, from supporting veterans with physical injuries and psychological scars to helping them reintegrate into civilian life and find spiritual healing. Through their compassionate presence, counseling, and faith-based activities, chaplains offer veterans the guidance and support they need to heal and thrive. The following chapters will delve deeper into the practical aspects of VA Chaplaincy, exploring the daily responsibilities and the impact of this crucial ministry on the veteran community.

## BUILDING TRUST

# Introduction

Building trust with veterans is a cornerstone of effective VA Chaplaincy. Many veterans may be skeptical of institutional support due to past experiences or the inherent nature of military culture, which often values self-reliance and resilience. Establishing trust is crucial for chaplains to provide meaningful spiritual and emotional care. This chapter explores the importance of building trust with veterans, the challenges involved, and strategies that VA Chaplains use to foster trust and rapport.

# The Importance of Trust

## *A Foundation for Healing*

### Emotional Safety

Trust creates a safe emotional space where veterans feel comfortable sharing their struggles, fears, and hopes. This safety is essential for effective counseling and spiritual guidance, as it allows veterans to open up and engage in the healing process.

### Effective Support

When veterans trust their chaplain, they are more likely to participate in counseling sessions, attend spiritual programs, and follow through with recommended interventions. Trust enhances the effectiveness of the chaplain's support, leading to better outcomes for the veteran.

Building Relationships

Trust is the foundation of any strong relationship. For VA Chaplains, building a trusting relationship with veterans is critical to providing ongoing support and fostering a sense of community and belonging.

# Challenges in Building Trust

## Skepticism of Institutional Support

Past Negative Experiences

Many veterans have had negative experiences with institutions, including healthcare systems, government agencies, and even the military itself. These experiences can lead to a deep-seated skepticism and reluctance to engage with institutional support services.

Military Culture

Military culture often emphasizes strength, self-reliance, and stoicism. Veterans may view seeking help as a sign of weakness, making them hesitant to trust or rely on others, including chaplains.

## Diverse Backgrounds

## Cultural and Religious Differences

Veterans come from diverse cultural and religious backgrounds, which can influence their perceptions and expectations of spiritual care. Chaplains must navigate these differences with sensitivity and respect to build trust.

### Varied Experiences

The experiences of veterans can vary widely, from those who served in combat to those who had non-combat roles. These varied experiences shape veterans' needs and perspectives, requiring chaplains to adopt a personalized approach to building trust.

# Strategies for Building Trust

## *Demonstrating Genuine Care and Empathy*

### Active Listening

Active listening is a fundamental skill for building trust. Chaplains demonstrate genuine care by listening attentively to veterans' stories, validating their experiences, and showing empathy. This approach helps veterans feel heard and understood.

### Consistency and Reliability

Being consistent and reliable in their interactions helps chaplains build trust. Veterans need to know that they can count on their chaplain to be there for them, whether for regular counseling sessions, during crises, or simply for a chat.

## Respecting Autonomy and Empowerment

### Respecting Veterans' Choices

Respecting veterans' autonomy and decisions is crucial for building trust. Chaplains must avoid being judgmental or directive, instead supporting veterans in making their own choices about their spiritual and emotional care.

### Empowering Veterans

Empowering veterans by involving them in their own care plan fosters trust. Chaplains can help veterans set personal goals, develop coping strategies, and take an active role in their healing process. This empowerment reinforces veterans' sense of control and self-efficacy.

## Building Cultural Competence

### Cultural Sensitivity

Cultural competence involves understanding and respecting the cultural backgrounds and beliefs of veterans. Chaplains must educate themselves about different cultural practices and religious traditions to provide inclusive and respectful care.

### Personalized Care

Personalizing care to meet the unique needs and preferences of each veteran is essential. This may involve adapting spiritual practices, offering interfaith support, or acknowledging and incorporating veterans' cultural heritage into their care.

## *Transparency and Honesty*

### Clear Communication

Clear and honest communication is vital for building trust. Chaplains should be transparent about their role, the services they provide, and the limits of confidentiality. This openness helps veterans understand what to expect and reduces uncertainty.

### Addressing Concerns

When veterans express concerns or skepticism, chaplains should address these issues directly and honestly. Acknowledging past negative experiences and showing a willingness to understand and rectify them can help build trust.

# Case Studies and Examples

## *Case Study: Building Trust with a Combat Veteran*

### Initial Skepticism

John, a combat veteran, was initially skeptical of institutional support due to past negative experiences with the VA healthcare system. He was reluctant to engage with his chaplain, feeling that opening up would make him appear weak.

### Building Rapport

John's chaplain took a patient and consistent approach, regularly checking in and offering support without being intrusive. Over time, John began to appreciate the chaplain's genuine concern and reliability.

Gaining Trust

Through active listening and respecting John's autonomy, the chaplain gradually built trust. John started attending counseling sessions and participating in group activities, finding solace and support in the chaplain's guidance.

## *Example: Cultural Sensitivity in Practice*

Understanding Diverse Beliefs

Maria, a chaplain with a diverse caseload, made it a priority to understand the cultural and religious backgrounds of the veterans she served. She attended cultural competency workshops and engaged in discussions with veterans to learn about their traditions.

Personalized Spiritual Care

When working with a Native American veteran, Maria incorporated traditional practices such as smudging and talking circles into their sessions. This personalized approach helped the veteran feel respected and understood, building a strong foundation of trust.

# The Impact of Trust

*Enhanced Healing and Recovery*

Improved Engagement

When veterans trust their chaplain, they are more likely to engage fully in the healing process. This engagement leads to better participation in counseling, spiritual activities, and rehabilitation programs, ultimately enhancing their recovery.

Emotional and Spiritual Growth

Trust fosters a safe environment for veterans to explore their emotions and spiritual beliefs. This exploration promotes emotional healing and spiritual growth, helping veterans find peace and purpose.

## Strengthening Community

Building Connections

Trust between chaplains and veterans helps build a sense of community. Veterans who trust their chaplain are more likely to participate in group activities, support each other, and create a network of mutual aid and encouragement.

Long-Term Support

A trusting relationship with a chaplain provides veterans with long-term support. This ongoing connection ensures that veterans have a reliable source of spiritual and emotional care, even as their needs evolve over time.

# Conclusion

Building trust with veterans is essential for VA Chaplains to provide effective spiritual and emotional support. The process involves overcoming skepticism, respecting autonomy, demonstrating genuine care, and being culturally competent. Through these strategies, chaplains create a foundation of trust that enhances veterans' healing, fosters community, and supports their long-term well-being. The following chapters will delve deeper into the practical aspects of VA Chaplaincy, exploring the daily responsibilities and the impact of this crucial ministry on the veteran community.

## PRACTICAL MINISTRY

# Introduction

Practical ministry is at the heart of VA Chaplaincy, encompassing a wide range of activities designed to support the spiritual and emotional well-being of veterans. From hospital visits and memorial services to one-on-one counseling sessions, these activities provide essential care and connection. This chapter explores various practical ministry activities, offering examples and insights into how VA Chaplains serve those who have served.

# Hospital Visits

## *The Importance of Bedside Ministry*

Providing Comfort and Support

Hospital visits are a crucial aspect of chaplaincy, offering veterans comfort and support during times of illness or recovery. Chaplains visit veterans at their bedside, providing a reassuring presence and emotional support.

Spiritual Care

During hospital visits, chaplains offer spiritual care tailored to the needs of the veteran. This can include prayer, reading scripture, or simply sitting in silent companionship. The goal is to provide a sense of peace and spiritual connection.

## *Example: Visiting a Veteran with Chronic Illness*

Initial Visit

Chaplain David regularly visits Tom, a veteran with a chronic illness. On his first visit, David introduced himself, listened to Tom's story, and offered a prayer for his healing and comfort. Tom, initially reserved, appreciated the chaplain's gentle approach.

Ongoing Support

Over time, David's visits became a source of comfort for Tom. They discussed Tom's fears and hopes, shared prayers, and read inspirational passages from the Bible. David's consistent presence provided Tom with spiritual strength and emotional support, enhancing his overall well-being.

# Memorial Services

## *Honoring the Fallen*

The Role of Memorial Services

Memorial services are a solemn and significant part of a chaplain's ministry. These services honor the lives and sacrifices of veterans who have passed away, providing a space for families and friends to grieve and find closure.



Chaplains work closely with families to plan memorial services that reflect the wishes and beliefs of the deceased. This involves selecting readings, music, and rituals that hold special meaning for the family.

## *Example: A Memorial Service for a World War II Veteran*

Family Consultation

When Jack, a World War II veteran, passed away, Chaplain Maria met with his family to plan the memorial service. They shared stories about Jack's life, his faith, and his love for hymns. Maria helped the family select hymns and readings that honored Jack's legacy.

The Service

On the day of the service, Maria led a heartfelt ceremony that included scripture readings, hymns, and personal reflections from family members. Her words of comfort and the inclusive nature of the service provided solace to Jack's grieving family, helping them celebrate his life and service.

# One-on-One Counseling Sessions

*Providing Personal Support*

## The Counseling Process

One-on-one counseling sessions are a key component of a chaplain's ministry, offering veterans a private and safe space to discuss their struggles, fears, and spiritual questions. Chaplains use active listening, empathy, and spiritual guidance to support veterans in their healing journey.

### Addressing Specific Needs

Each counseling session is tailored to the individual needs of the veteran, whether they are dealing with PTSD, moral injury, grief, or other challenges. Chaplains provide personalized care that addresses both emotional and spiritual needs.

## *Example: Counseling a Veteran with PTSD*

### Initial Session

Chaplain Sarah began working with Mike, a veteran struggling with PTSD. During their first session, Sarah created a safe and non-judgmental space for Mike to share his experiences. She listened attentively, validated his feelings, and offered spiritual support.

### Ongoing Sessions

Over several months, Sarah and Mike worked together through regular counseling sessions. Sarah used a combination of spiritual practices, such as prayer and meditation, and practical techniques, like breathing exercises, to help Mike manage his PTSD symptoms. Through their sessions, Mike began to find a sense of peace and hope, improving his quality of life.

# Leading Worship Services

## Creating a Spiritual Community

Types of Services

Chaplains lead a variety of worship services to meet the diverse spiritual needs of veterans. These can include traditional religious services, interfaith gatherings, and special ceremonies for holidays or significant events.

The Importance of Worship

Worship services provide veterans with a sense of community, spiritual nourishment, and continuity. They offer a regular opportunity for veterans to connect with their faith and with others who share similar beliefs.

## Example: An Interfaith Worship Service

Planning the Service

Chaplain James organized an interfaith worship service to celebrate Veterans Day. He collaborated with representatives from different faith traditions to create a service that was inclusive and respectful of all beliefs.

Conducting the Service

The service included prayers, readings, and reflections from various religious traditions, along with music and moments of silent reflection. Veterans from different backgrounds participated, finding common ground in their shared experiences and faith. The service fostered a sense of unity and mutual respect, reinforcing the importance of spiritual community.

# Group Activities and Support Programs

## *Building Connections and Support*

Support Groups

Chaplains facilitate support groups that provide veterans with a space to share their experiences, offer mutual support, and engage in spiritual practices. These groups can focus on specific issues, such as PTSD, grief, or moral injury, or provide general support and fellowship.

Spiritual Retreats

Spiritual retreats offer veterans an opportunity to step away from their daily routines and engage in intensive spiritual reflection and renewal. Chaplains organize and lead retreats that include prayer, meditation, discussions, and recreational activities.

## *Example: A PTSD Support Group*

Chaplain Maria established a PTSD support group for veterans in her care. She invited veterans to join the group, emphasizing the importance of mutual support and shared experiences.

Group Sessions

During group sessions, veterans shared their stories, discussed coping strategies, and participated in group prayers and meditations. Maria facilitated discussions, provided spiritual insights, and offered encouragement. The support group became a vital source of strength and connection for its members, helping them navigate their challenges together.

# Community Outreach and Engagement

## *Extending Support Beyond the VA*

Community Partnerships

Chaplains often collaborate with local religious organizations, community groups, and veteran service organizations to extend their support beyond the VA. These partnerships provide additional resources and opportunities for veterans to connect with their communities.

Public Speaking and Advocacy

Chaplains engage in public speaking and advocacy to raise awareness about the needs of veterans and the importance of spiritual care. They speak at community events, participate in panel discussions, and advocate for policies that support veterans' well-being.

## *Example: Partnering with a Local Church*

Establishing the Partnership

Chaplain David partnered with a local church to provide additional support for veterans. The church offered space for support group meetings and organized community events for veterans and their families.

Community Events

David and the church's pastor organized events such as community dinners, holiday celebrations, and volunteer opportunities. These events helped veterans feel connected to their community, provided a supportive environment for their families, and fostered a sense of belonging.

# Conclusion

Practical ministry activities are the lifeblood of VA Chaplaincy, providing essential support to veterans through hospital visits, memorial services, one-on-one counseling sessions, worship services, group activities, and community outreach. These activities offer comfort, spiritual nourishment, and a sense of community, helping veterans navigate their challenges and find healing and hope. The following chapters will continue to explore the various aspects of VA Chaplaincy, highlighting the impact of this crucial ministry on the veteran community.

# CHAPTER 05



## HEALING AFTER SERVICE

## THE SPIRITUAL PATH TO HEALING

## Introduction

For many veterans, the journey to healing after service involves more than just addressing physical injuries and psychological wounds; it also requires spiritual healing. Spiritual practices such as prayer, meditation, and religious rituals can play a crucial role in this process, providing veterans with comfort, hope, and a sense of purpose. This chapter explores how these practices aid in the healing process and highlights the ways VA Chaplains facilitate spiritual healing for veterans.

## The Role of Spiritual Practices in Healing

*Prayer*

The Power of Prayer

Prayer is a powerful tool for spiritual healing, offering veterans a direct line of communication with a higher power. It provides a sense of connection, comfort, and reassurance, helping veterans feel supported and understood in their struggles.

Types of Prayer

Different types of prayer can be used to address various needs:

- **Petitionary Prayer:** Asking for specific help or guidance.
- **Intercessory Prayer:** Praying on behalf of others.
- **Thanksgiving Prayer:** Expressing gratitude.
- **Contemplative Prayer:** Focusing on a deep, reflective connection with the divine.

## *Meditation*

Benefits of Meditation

Meditation offers numerous benefits, including reduced stress, increased emotional resilience, and improved mental clarity. For veterans, meditation can be a way to calm the mind, manage symptoms of PTSD, and cultivate inner peace.

Types of Meditation

Several types of meditation can be particularly beneficial for veterans:

- **Mindfulness Meditation:** Focusing on the present moment and cultivating awareness.

- **Loving-Kindness Meditation:** Generating feelings of compassion and love toward oneself and others.
- **Guided Imagery:** Using visualization to promote relaxation and healing.

## Religious Rituals

### The Importance of Rituals

Religious rituals provide structure and a sense of continuity, offering veterans a way to express their faith and connect with their spiritual community. Rituals can mark significant life events, provide comfort during difficult times, and foster a sense of belonging.

### Examples of Rituals

Common religious rituals that support healing include:

- **Sacraments:** Such as communion or baptism, which provide spiritual nourishment.
- **Candle Lighting:** Symbolizing hope and remembrance.
- **Anointing of the Sick:** Offering prayers and blessings for healing.
- **Fasting and Feasting:** Observing religious fasts or communal meals that strengthen spiritual discipline and community bonds.

# The Chaplain's Role in Facilitating Spiritual Healing

## Providing Spiritual Guidance

## One-on-One Counseling

VA Chaplains offer one-on-one spiritual counseling to veterans, helping them explore their faith, address spiritual questions, and find meaning in their experiences. These sessions provide a safe space for veterans to discuss their beliefs and receive personalized guidance.

## Group Sessions

Chaplains also facilitate group sessions where veterans can share their spiritual journeys, support one another, and engage in collective spiritual practices. These sessions foster a sense of community and mutual support.

# Leading Spiritual Practices

## Prayer Groups

Chaplains organize and lead prayer groups, providing veterans with regular opportunities to pray together and support each other spiritually. These groups can focus on specific needs, such as praying for healing, strength, or guidance.

## Meditation Workshops

Chaplains conduct meditation workshops, teaching veterans different meditation techniques and providing guided sessions. These workshops help veterans incorporate meditation into their daily routines, promoting long-term mental and emotional well-being.

Chaplains conduct religious rituals that are meaningful to veterans, such as communion services, candlelight vigils, and anointing ceremonies. These rituals offer spiritual comfort and help veterans feel connected to their faith community.

# Case Studies of Spiritual Healing

## *Case Study: Healing Through Prayer*

John's Journey

John, a veteran struggling with severe PTSD, found solace through prayer. Initially skeptical, John began attending prayer sessions led by his chaplain, David. Through regular participation, John discovered a sense of peace and strength that helped him manage his symptoms.

Impact of Prayer

Prayer provided John with a way to express his fears and hopes, helping him feel connected to a higher power and supported in his healing journey. Over time, John's faith grew stronger, and his PTSD symptoms became more manageable, illustrating the profound impact of prayer on his recovery.

## *Case Study: The Power of Meditation*

## Maria's Experience

Maria, a veteran dealing with anxiety and depression, was introduced to mindfulness meditation by her chaplain, Sarah. Initially, Maria struggled to quiet her mind, but with Sarah's guidance, she learned to focus on her breath and stay present in the moment.

## Benefits of Meditation

Meditation helped Maria reduce her anxiety, improve her mood, and gain greater control over her thoughts. The practice became a cornerstone of her daily routine, providing a sense of calm and clarity that significantly enhanced her overall well-being.

# Case Study: Finding Comfort in Rituals

## Tom's Story

Tom, a veteran coping with chronic illness, found comfort in participating in religious rituals. Chaplain James conducted regular anointing ceremonies and candlelight vigils, which Tom found deeply comforting and spiritually uplifting.

## Impact of Rituals

These rituals provided Tom with a sense of peace and connection to his faith community. They helped him find meaning and hope in his illness, illustrating the healing power of religious rituals in his life.

# Incorporating Spiritual Practices into Daily Life

## Developing a Routine

### Establishing Consistency

Chaplains encourage veterans to incorporate spiritual practices into their daily routines. Establishing a consistent practice, whether it's daily prayer, meditation, or participating in rituals, helps reinforce the benefits and makes these practices an integral part of their lives.

### Creating a Sacred Space

Veterans are encouraged to create a sacred space in their homes where they can engage in spiritual practices. This space can be a quiet corner with meaningful symbols, such as candles, religious texts, or items that hold personal significance.

## Engaging with the Community

### Joining Faith-Based Groups

Veterans are encouraged to join faith-based groups or communities where they can share their spiritual journey and receive support. These groups provide a sense of belonging and mutual encouragement, enhancing the healing process.

Participating in Community Activities

Engaging in community activities, such as volunteer work or attending religious services, helps veterans stay connected to their faith community and contribute positively to society. These activities foster a sense of purpose and fulfillment.

# The Long-Term Benefits of Spiritual Healing

## *Sustaining Mental and Emotional Well-Being*

Ongoing Support

Spiritual practices provide ongoing support for veterans, helping them maintain their mental and emotional well-being over the long term. Regular engagement in these practices offers a stable foundation for coping with life's challenges.

Building Resilience

Spiritual healing builds resilience, enabling veterans to navigate future difficulties with greater strength and confidence. The skills and insights gained through spiritual practices empower veterans to face adversity with hope and determination.

## *Enhancing Quality of Life*

Finding Peace and Purpose

Spiritual healing helps veterans find peace and purpose, enhancing their overall quality of life. By connecting with their faith and engaging in meaningful practices, veterans can experience a deeper sense of fulfillment and joy.



Spiritual practices also strengthen veterans' relationships with their families and communities. The emotional and spiritual growth fostered by these practices enhances their ability to connect with others, fostering stronger and more supportive relationships.

# Conclusion

The spiritual path to healing is a vital component of recovery for many veterans. Through practices such as prayer, meditation, and religious rituals, veterans can find comfort, strength, and a sense of purpose. VA Chaplains play a crucial role in facilitating these practices, providing guidance and support to help veterans navigate their spiritual journeys. By incorporating these practices into their daily lives, veterans can experience profound healing and long-term well-being, enriching their lives and enhancing their resilience. The following chapters will continue to explore the various aspects of VA Chaplaincy, highlighting the impact of this crucial ministry on the veteran community.

## CASE STUDIES

# Introduction

VA Chaplains play a pivotal role in the healing journey of veterans, offering spiritual guidance, emotional support, and practical assistance. This chapter presents several case studies of veterans who have found profound healing through the dedicated support of their VA Chaplains. These stories illustrate the transformative impact of chaplaincy on the lives of those who have served.

# Case Study 1: John's Journey with PTSD

## *Background*

Initial Struggles

John, a combat veteran, returned home with severe PTSD. He experienced debilitating flashbacks, nightmares, and intense anxiety. These symptoms made it difficult for him to maintain relationships and hold down a job, leading to feelings of isolation and hopelessness.

Seeking Help

Reluctant at first, John sought help after a fellow veteran recommended speaking with a VA Chaplain. He was introduced to Chaplain David, who had extensive experience working with PTSD patients.

## *The Chaplain's Approach*

Building Trust

David's first step was to build trust with John. He offered a safe, non-judgmental space where John could share his experiences and fears. David's consistent presence and empathetic listening helped John feel understood and supported.

Spiritual Counseling

David introduced John to spiritual counseling, incorporating prayer and scripture reading into their sessions. These practices provided John with a sense of peace and connection to a higher power, which helped alleviate some of his anxiety.

## The Healing Process

Coping Strategies

David taught John various coping strategies, including mindfulness meditation and breathing exercises, to manage his PTSD symptoms. These techniques helped John gain better control over his reactions and reduce the intensity of his flashbacks.

Group Support

John also joined a PTSD support group facilitated by David. Sharing his experiences with other veterans who faced similar challenges helped John feel less isolated and more supported.

## Outcome

Improved Mental Health

Over time, John's symptoms significantly improved. He experienced fewer flashbacks and nightmares and began to rebuild his relationships and find stability in his daily life. The combination of spiritual counseling, coping strategies, and group support played a crucial role in his recovery.

Renewed Purpose

John found a renewed sense of purpose through his faith and community. He became an active member of his church and started volunteering, helping other veterans navigate their own healing journeys. John's story is a testament to the transformative power of chaplaincy in addressing PTSD.

# Case Study 2: Maria's Path to Overcoming Grief

## *Background*

A Deep Loss

Maria, a retired Navy officer, lost her husband, who was also a veteran, to cancer. The loss left her devastated, struggling with profound grief and a sense of emptiness. She withdrew from her social circles and experienced severe depression.

Reaching Out

At the urging of her children, Maria reached out to Chaplain Sarah, seeking support to cope with her loss. Sarah's compassionate approach provided Maria with the comfort and guidance she desperately needed.

## *The Chaplain's Approach*

Grief Counseling

Sarah provided grief counseling, helping Maria navigate the complex emotions associated with her loss. Through regular sessions, Sarah helped Maria express her grief, acknowledge her pain, and begin the healing process.

Rituals of Remembrance

Sarah introduced Maria to rituals of remembrance, such as lighting candles in memory of her husband and creating a memory book filled with photos and stories. These rituals provided Maria with a way to honor her husband's memory and find solace in her grief.

## The Healing Process

Spiritual Practices

Sarah encouraged Maria to engage in spiritual practices that brought her comfort, such as prayer and attending church services. These practices helped Maria reconnect with her faith and find strength in her spirituality.

Community Support

Maria joined a grief support group led by Sarah. Sharing her experiences with others who had lost loved ones helped Maria feel less alone and more understood. The support group became a vital part of her healing journey.

## Outcome

Emotional Healing

With Sarah's support, Maria gradually began to heal emotionally. She found ways to cope with her grief and started to regain a sense of normalcy in her life. Maria's depression lifted, and she became more engaged with her family and community.

### Honoring Her Husband's Legacy

Maria found purpose in honoring her husband's legacy by volunteering at a veterans' organization. She helped organize events and support groups, using her experience to help others navigate their own grief. Maria's journey illustrates the profound impact of compassionate chaplaincy on overcoming loss.

# Case Study 3: Tom's Battle with Moral Injury

## *Background*

### A Heavy Burden

Tom, a veteran who served in multiple combat tours, struggled with moral injury. He was haunted by actions he took during combat that conflicted with his moral and ethical beliefs. This led to deep feelings of guilt, shame, and spiritual distress.

### Seeking Redemption

Tom sought help from Chaplain James, hoping to find forgiveness and peace. James had a background in ethics and moral theology, making him well-suited to address Tom's concerns.

## *The Chaplain's Approach*

Exploring Moral Injury

James helped Tom explore the concept of moral injury, explaining that his feelings of guilt and shame were common among veterans and that they could be addressed through spiritual healing and forgiveness.

Facilitating Forgiveness

James guided Tom through a process of seeking forgiveness, both from himself and a higher power. They engaged in reflective conversations, prayer, and scriptural study to help Tom find a path to redemption.

## The Healing Process

Spiritual Exercises

James introduced Tom to spiritual exercises, such as journaling and contemplative prayer, to help him process his emotions and find clarity. These exercises provided Tom with tools to manage his guilt and begin the healing process.

Community Engagement

Tom began participating in community service activities organized by James. Helping others gave Tom a sense of purpose and allowed him to make amends for his past actions in a meaningful way.

## Outcome

Finding Peace

Through James' guidance, Tom found a sense of peace and forgiveness. He learned to accept his past actions and focus on the positive impact he could have in the present. Tom's spiritual journey helped him reconcile his beliefs with his experiences, leading to profound healing.

A New Mission

Tom became an advocate for other veterans dealing with moral injury, sharing his story and providing support. His journey from guilt to redemption serves as a powerful example of the healing power of chaplaincy.

# Case Study 4: Anna's Recovery from Depression

## *Background*

Struggling with Transition

Anna, an Air Force veteran, struggled with depression after transitioning to civilian life. She felt disconnected from her military community and found it difficult to adapt to her new environment. Her depression affected her relationships and overall well-being.

Seeking Help

Anna decided to seek help from Chaplain Maria, who was known for her empathetic approach and experience in mental health support.

## The Chaplain's Approach

Building a Connection

Maria focused on building a strong connection with Anna, offering a safe and supportive space for her to share her struggles. This connection was crucial in helping Anna feel understood and supported.

Integrating Faith

Maria helped Anna integrate her faith into her healing journey. They engaged in regular prayer sessions and discussed how Anna's spiritual beliefs could provide strength and guidance during challenging times.

## The Healing Process

Therapeutic Techniques

Maria introduced Anna to therapeutic techniques such as mindfulness meditation and cognitive-behavioral strategies. These techniques helped Anna manage her depressive symptoms and develop healthier thought patterns.

Social Engagement

Maria encouraged Anna to engage in social activities and reconnect with her community. She introduced Anna to a veterans' group and helped her find volunteer opportunities that aligned with her interests.

## Outcome

Improved Mental Health

Anna's depression symptoms gradually improved through a combination of spiritual guidance, therapeutic techniques, and social engagement. She regained a sense of purpose and started building positive relationships.

Empowered to Help Others

Anna's journey inspired her to help other veterans facing similar struggles. She became a peer mentor in the veterans' group, offering support and sharing her experiences. Anna's story highlights the importance of holistic chaplaincy in addressing mental health challenges.

# Conclusion

These case studies illustrate the transformative impact of VA Chaplaincy on the lives of veterans. Through spiritual guidance, emotional support, and practical assistance, chaplains help veterans navigate their healing journeys, addressing issues such as PTSD, grief, moral injury, and depression. The dedicated support of chaplains not only aids in individual recovery but also empowers veterans to contribute positively to their communities. The following chapters will continue to explore the various aspects of VA Chaplaincy, highlighting the profound and lasting impact of this crucial ministry on the veteran community.

## THE ROLE OF COMMUNITY

# Introduction

Community plays a vital role in the healing process for veterans. The sense of belonging, mutual support, and shared experiences found within a community can significantly enhance emotional and spiritual well-being. This chapter highlights the importance of community in the healing journey, focusing on support groups, faith-based community programs, and the broader network of relationships that contribute to veterans' recovery.

# The Importance of Community in Healing

## *A Sense of Belonging*

### Overcoming Isolation

Many veterans experience isolation after leaving the military, struggling to find a sense of belonging in civilian life. Community provides a network of support and connection, helping veterans overcome feelings of loneliness and disconnection.

### Shared Experiences

Being part of a community of fellow veterans allows individuals to share their experiences with others who understand their journey. This shared understanding fosters empathy, support, and camaraderie, essential for emotional healing.

## *Emotional and Practical Support*

Mutual Support

Community groups offer mutual support, where veterans can give and receive encouragement, advice, and assistance. This reciprocity strengthens bonds and reinforces the idea that no one has to face their challenges alone.

Access to Resources

Communities often provide access to resources such as counseling services, job placement programs, and educational opportunities. These resources are crucial for veterans transitioning to civilian life and seeking stability and growth.

# Support Groups

## The Structure of Support Groups

Peer-Led Groups

Many support groups are peer-led, meaning they are facilitated by veterans who have undergone similar experiences. This peer leadership fosters trust and relatability, encouraging open and honest discussions.

Professional-Led Groups

Some support groups are led by professionals, such as VA Chaplains or mental health counselors. These groups provide a more structured environment, with guided discussions and therapeutic interventions tailored to the participants' needs.

## The Benefits of Support Groups

Emotional Expression

Support groups provide a safe space for veterans to express their emotions, share their stories, and discuss their challenges. This expression is crucial for processing trauma and fostering emotional resilience.

Building Coping Skills

Through group discussions and activities, veterans can learn and share coping skills. These skills help them manage stress, anxiety, and other emotional difficulties more effectively.

Reducing Stigma

Participating in support groups helps reduce the stigma associated with seeking help. Veterans see that others face similar challenges and that it is okay to seek support and talk about their struggles.

## *Example: PTSD Support Group*

The Group's Formation

Chaplain Sarah formed a PTSD support group at a local VA facility. The group met weekly and was open to any veteran struggling with PTSD symptoms.

The Group's Impact

Members of the group found solace in sharing their experiences and learning coping strategies from one another. The sense of community and understanding helped reduce their feelings of isolation and provided them with practical tools to manage their symptoms. Over time, many group members reported significant improvements in their emotional well-being.

# Faith-Based Community Programs

## *The Role of Faith in Community*

### Spiritual Connection

Faith-based community programs provide a spiritual connection that many veterans find comforting and strengthening. These programs offer opportunities for worship, prayer, and other spiritual practices that foster a sense of peace and purpose.

### Moral and Ethical Support

Faith communities often provide moral and ethical support, helping veterans reconcile their experiences with their beliefs. This support is crucial for those struggling with moral injury or spiritual questions.

## *Types of Faith-Based Programs*

### Worship Services

Regular worship services provide a communal space for veterans to practice their faith and find spiritual nourishment. These services offer continuity and a sense of belonging, reinforcing the veterans' spiritual foundation.

Bible Studies and Religious Education

Bible studies and religious education classes offer veterans a chance to deepen their understanding of their faith. These programs often include discussions about how faith can help address life's challenges, providing veterans with spiritual tools for coping and growth.

Service and Outreach Programs

Many faith-based communities organize service and outreach programs where veterans can volunteer and help others. Participating in these programs provides a sense of purpose and fulfillment, enhancing veterans' own healing while making a positive impact on their community.

## Example: A Church-Based Veterans Group

Formation and Goals

Chaplain James collaborated with a local church to form a veterans group that met for weekly Bible studies and fellowship. The group aimed to provide spiritual support and foster a sense of community among veteran members.

Activities and Impact

The group engaged in various activities, including Bible studies, prayer meetings, and community service projects. Members reported feeling more connected to their faith and to each other. The group's support helped them navigate their challenges and find meaning and purpose in their post-military lives.

# Broader Community Networks

## Integration into Civilian Life

### Social Clubs and Organizations

Social clubs and organizations, such as the American Legion or Veterans of Foreign Wars (VFW), provide veterans with additional opportunities to connect with peers, participate in social activities, and engage in community service. These organizations help veterans integrate into civilian life while maintaining a connection to their military identity.

### Educational and Employment Support

Community networks often include resources for education and employment, helping veterans acquire new skills, pursue further education, and find meaningful employment. These opportunities are essential for veterans seeking to build stable and fulfilling civilian lives.

## Family and Friends

### Rebuilding Relationships

Family and friends are a crucial part of the broader community network. Rebuilding and maintaining strong relationships with loved ones provide emotional support and stability for veterans. Chaplains often work with families to facilitate open communication and mutual understanding, helping to strengthen these bonds.

Caregivers, often family members, play a significant role in supporting veterans. Community programs that provide support and resources for caregivers help them manage their responsibilities and maintain their own well-being, ensuring they can continue to provide effective care.

# Case Study: The Impact of Community on Healing

## John's Journey

### Initial Struggles

John, a combat veteran, struggled with PTSD and depression after leaving the military. He felt isolated and disconnected from his family and community, which exacerbated his symptoms.

### Finding Support

John joined a PTSD support group led by Chaplain David and became involved in his local church's veterans group. These communities provided him with the support and understanding he needed to begin his healing journey.

## The Healing Process

Group Support

Through the PTSD support group, John learned coping strategies and found solace in sharing his experiences with others who understood his struggles. The group's mutual support helped John feel less isolated and more hopeful.

Faith-Based Programs

John's involvement in the church's veterans group strengthened his faith and provided him with spiritual guidance. The group's activities, such as Bible studies and community service projects, helped John find purpose and fulfillment.

## *Outcome*

Improved Well-Being

With the support of these communities, John's PTSD symptoms and depression significantly improved. He developed stronger relationships with his family, found meaningful work through a veterans employment program, and became an active member of his community.

Giving Back

John's journey inspired him to give back. He became a peer mentor in the PTSD support group and a volunteer leader in the church's veterans group, using his experiences to help other veterans navigate their own healing journeys.

# Conclusion

Community plays a crucial role in the healing process for veterans. Whether through support groups, faith-based programs, or broader community networks, the sense of belonging, mutual support, and shared experiences found in these communities significantly enhance emotional and spiritual well-being. VA Chaplains facilitate these connections, helping veterans find the support they need to heal and thrive. The following chapters will continue to explore the various aspects of VA Chaplaincy, highlighting the profound and lasting impact of this crucial ministry on the veteran community.

# CHAPTER 06

## THE VETERANS SHEPHERD

## PASTORAL CARE IN THE VA

## Introduction

Pastoral care within the Veterans Affairs (VA) system is a unique and vital aspect of supporting veterans' spiritual and emotional well-being. While it shares many elements with traditional church-based pastoral care, the VA setting presents distinct challenges and opportunities that require specialized approaches. This chapter details the pastoral care practices employed by VA Chaplains, highlighting how they cater to the specific needs of veterans and how these practices differ from those in traditional church settings.

# The Unique Context of VA Pastoral Care

*Understanding the Veteran Population*

Diverse Backgrounds

Veterans come from diverse cultural, religious, and socioeconomic backgrounds. They bring with them a wide range of experiences, from different branches of the military and various conflicts. This diversity requires chaplains to be adaptable and culturally competent in their pastoral care approach.

Complex Needs

Veterans often have complex needs, including physical injuries, PTSD, moral injury, and other psychological issues. These needs require a holistic approach to care that addresses the physical, emotional, and spiritual aspects of healing.

## The VA Setting

Institutional Environment

The VA operates within a large, institutional environment that includes hospitals, outpatient clinics, and long-term care facilities. This setting differs significantly from the more intimate and community-based environment of a traditional church, necessitating different pastoral care strategies.

Interdisciplinary Collaboration

VA Chaplains work as part of an interdisciplinary team that includes medical professionals, psychologists, social workers, and other specialists. This collaborative approach ensures comprehensive care for veterans but also requires chaplains to navigate and integrate their spiritual care within the broader healthcare system.

# Pastoral Care Practices in the VA

## *Holistic Assessment and Care Planning*

### Spiritual Assessments

VA Chaplains conduct spiritual assessments to understand the unique spiritual needs and resources of each veteran. These assessments include discussions about the veteran's faith background, spiritual practices, and current concerns. The information gathered helps chaplains tailor their care to each individual.

### Integrated Care Plans

Based on the spiritual assessment, chaplains develop integrated care plans that address the spiritual, emotional, and psychological needs of veterans. These plans are coordinated with the broader healthcare team to ensure that all aspects of the veteran's well-being are considered.

## *One-on-One Counseling*

### Personalized Support

One-on-one counseling sessions provide personalized support for veterans. Chaplains offer a safe and confidential space for veterans to discuss their struggles, fears, and spiritual questions. These sessions are tailored to the individual's needs, whether they are dealing with grief, moral injury, PTSD, or other issues.

In these sessions, chaplains provide spiritual guidance, helping veterans explore their faith, find meaning in their experiences, and develop coping strategies. Prayer, scripture reading, and reflective conversation are common elements of these counseling sessions.

## Group Therapy and Support

Peer Support Groups

Chaplains facilitate peer support groups where veterans can share their experiences and support each other. These groups often focus on specific issues, such as PTSD, grief, or moral injury, providing a sense of community and mutual understanding.

Therapeutic Groups

In collaboration with mental health professionals, chaplains lead therapeutic groups that incorporate spiritual care into evidence-based therapeutic practices. These groups might include activities like meditation, mindfulness, and art therapy, integrated with spiritual reflections and discussions.

## Crisis Intervention

Immediate Support

VA Chaplains are often called upon to provide immediate support during crises, such as suicidal ideation, acute grief, or severe anxiety attacks. They offer a calming presence, emotional support, and spiritual comfort, helping veterans navigate these difficult moments.

Coordination with Mental Health Services

Chaplains work closely with mental health services to ensure that veterans in crisis receive the comprehensive care they need. This collaboration ensures that spiritual care complements psychological and medical interventions.

# Differences from Traditional Church-Based Pastoral Care

## Setting and Structure

Institutional vs. Community-Based

Unlike traditional church settings, VA Chaplaincy operates within a large, institutional framework. This requires chaplains to navigate bureaucratic processes and collaborate with a wide range of professionals, which is less common in church-based pastoral care.

Flexibility in Worship

In the VA, chaplains must be flexible in their approach to worship and spiritual practices. Services may be conducted in hospital rooms, community rooms, or outdoor spaces, depending on the needs and capabilities of veterans. This flexibility contrasts with the more structured and predictable environment of a church.

## Scope of Care

Holistic Approach

VA Chaplains adopt a holistic approach to care, addressing the physical, emotional, and spiritual needs of veterans. This interdisciplinary model differs from the more singular focus on spiritual well-being typically found in church settings.

Focus on Trauma and Mental Health

The prevalence of trauma and mental health issues among veterans requires chaplains to have specialized training and skills in these areas. This focus on trauma-informed care and mental health is a distinct aspect of VA Chaplaincy that is not as prevalent in traditional church settings.

## Collaboration and Integration

Interdisciplinary Collaboration

VA Chaplains are integral members of interdisciplinary teams, working alongside healthcare providers to deliver comprehensive care. This collaboration requires chaplains to understand medical terminology, treatment plans, and the roles of other healthcare professionals, integrating their spiritual care within this broader context.

Comprehensive Documentation

Chaplains in the VA are required to document their interactions and care plans in the veteran's medical record. This documentation ensures continuity of care and provides valuable information for the healthcare team, a practice that is generally not required in church-based pastoral care.

# Case Study: Implementing Pastoral Care in the VA

## Background

### Veteran Profile

Paul, a Vietnam War veteran, struggled with chronic pain, PTSD, and feelings of isolation. He was admitted to a VA hospital for treatment and was referred to Chaplain Maria for spiritual care.

## Initial Assessment

### Conducting a Spiritual Assessment

Maria conducted a comprehensive spiritual assessment, learning about Paul's faith background, his current spiritual practices, and his specific concerns. She discovered that Paul felt disconnected from his faith community and struggled with guilt and anger related to his wartime experiences.

### Developing a Care Plan

Based on the assessment, Maria developed an integrated care plan that included one-on-one counseling sessions, participation in a PTSD support group, and involvement in spiritual practices that Paul found meaningful.

## Providing Care

One-on-One Counseling

In their counseling sessions, Maria helped Paul explore his feelings of guilt and anger, offering spiritual guidance and support. They prayed together, read scripture, and discussed ways to reconnect with his faith.

Group Support

Paul joined a PTSD support group facilitated by Maria. The group provided him with a sense of community and mutual understanding, helping him feel less isolated and more supported.

Spiritual Practices

Maria encouraged Paul to engage in spiritual practices such as prayer, meditation, and attending worship services. These practices helped Paul find peace and strength in his faith.

## *Outcome*

Improved Well-Being

Through Maria's holistic and integrated approach, Paul experienced significant improvements in his emotional and spiritual well-being. His PTSD symptoms became more manageable, and he felt a renewed sense of connection to his faith and community.

Enhanced Quality of Life

Paul's participation in the support group and spiritual practices improved his overall quality of life. He found purpose in helping other veterans in the group, sharing his experiences and offering support.

# Conclusion

Pastoral care in the VA setting is a unique and vital aspect of supporting veterans' spiritual and emotional well-being. VA Chaplains employ a holistic approach that addresses the diverse and complex needs of veterans, integrating their care within the broader healthcare system. This approach differs from traditional church-based pastoral care in its setting, scope, and collaboration with interdisciplinary teams. The dedicated work of VA Chaplains, as illustrated in the case study of Paul, demonstrates the profound impact of comprehensive pastoral care on the healing and well-being of veterans. The following chapters will continue to explore the various aspects of VA Chaplaincy, highlighting the importance and impact of this crucial ministry on the veteran community.

## PROVIDING HOPE AND COMFORT

# Introduction

In times of difficulty, the presence of hope and comfort can be transformative for veterans and their families. VA Chaplains play a crucial role in providing these essential elements, offering spiritual guidance, emotional support, and practical assistance. This chapter explores the various ways in which VA Chaplains provide hope and comfort, highlighting their impact on the lives of those they serve.

# The Importance of Hope and Comfort

## *Emotional Resilience*

### Building Strength

Hope and comfort are vital for building emotional resilience. They provide veterans and their families with the strength to face challenges, navigate hardships, and maintain a positive outlook despite difficult circumstances.

### Alleviating Despair

In the face of overwhelming stress, physical pain, or emotional turmoil, hope and comfort can alleviate feelings of despair. They help individuals find meaning and purpose, reducing the burden of their struggles.

## *Spiritual Well-Being*

### Connecting with Faith

For many veterans, connecting with their faith is a source of profound comfort and hope. Spiritual practices and beliefs offer a framework for understanding suffering and finding peace, which is crucial for overall well-being.

### Providing a Sense of Purpose

Hope and comfort often come from a sense of purpose and direction. VA Chaplains help veterans and their families identify and pursue meaningful goals, enhancing their spiritual well-being and quality of life.

# Ways VA Chaplains Provide Hope and Comfort

## Offering Spiritual Guidance

### Prayer and Meditation

Chaplains lead veterans and their families in prayer and meditation, offering spiritual solace and a sense of connection to a higher power. These practices can provide immediate relief from stress and anxiety, fostering a sense of peace.

*Example: Guided Prayer Sessions*

Chaplain David conducts guided prayer sessions for veterans in his care. These sessions include prayers for healing, strength, and comfort, tailored to the specific needs and beliefs of each veteran. The sessions provide a moment of calm and reflection, helping veterans feel supported and uplifted.

### Scripture and Inspirational Readings

Reading scriptures and inspirational texts can offer hope and comfort by providing wisdom and perspective. Chaplains select passages that resonate with veterans' experiences, helping them find solace and meaning in their faith traditions.

*Example: Personalized Scripture Reading*

Chaplain Maria regularly visits veterans in the hospital, offering to read passages from the Bible or other inspirational texts. She chooses readings that speak to their current struggles, offering messages of hope, perseverance, and divine support. These readings often bring comfort and a renewed sense of faith.

## Providing Emotional Support

### Active Listening

One of the most powerful ways chaplains provide comfort is through active listening. By giving veterans and their families a safe space to express their feelings and share their stories, chaplains validate their experiences and offer emotional relief.

*Example: One-on-One Conversations*

Chaplain Sarah spends time with veterans, engaging in one-on-one conversations where they can openly discuss their fears, frustrations, and hopes. Her attentive listening and empathetic responses help veterans feel heard and understood, reducing their emotional burden.

### Counseling and Therapy

Chaplains offer counseling and therapy to help veterans navigate complex emotions and mental health challenges. These sessions provide tools for coping with stress, managing symptoms of PTSD and depression, and fostering emotional resilience.

*Example: Grief Counseling*

Chaplain James provides grief counseling to families who have lost loved ones. Through compassionate conversations, he helps them process their grief, find ways to honor their loved ones, and gradually move toward healing. His support helps families navigate one of the most challenging times of their lives.

## *Facilitating Community and Connection*

### Support Groups

Chaplains facilitate support groups where veterans and their families can connect with others facing similar challenges. These groups provide a sense of community, mutual support, and shared understanding, which are essential for healing.

### *Example: Veteran Support Group*

Chaplain John leads a veteran support group that meets weekly. The group offers a safe space for veterans to share their experiences, discuss coping strategies, and support one another. The camaraderie and understanding within the group provide hope and comfort to its members.

### Faith-Based Community Programs

Faith-based community programs, such as worship services, Bible studies, and religious education classes, help veterans and their families engage with their faith and connect with others. These programs offer spiritual nourishment and a sense of belonging.

### *Example: Church Partnership*

Chaplain Maria partners with a local church to offer a range of faith-based programs for veterans and their families. These include weekly worship services, Bible study groups, and community service projects. The church community provides a supportive and welcoming environment, enhancing the spiritual and emotional well-being of participants.

## *Practical Assistance and Advocacy*

Navigating the VA System

Chaplains assist veterans and their families in navigating the often complex VA system. They help them access resources, understand their benefits, and advocate for their needs, reducing stress and uncertainty.

*Example: Resource Coordination*

Chaplain David helps veterans coordinate their care by connecting them with medical, psychological, and social services within the VA. He ensures they receive comprehensive support, addressing all aspects of their well-being. This practical assistance alleviates some of the burdens they face, providing a sense of security and hope.

Crisis Intervention

In times of crisis, chaplains provide immediate support and intervention. Whether dealing with suicidal ideation, severe anxiety, or a family emergency, chaplains offer a calming presence and practical assistance to help veterans and their families navigate the crisis.

*Example: Crisis Support*

Chaplain Sarah responds to a veteran experiencing a severe anxiety attack. She provides immediate emotional support, uses grounding techniques to help the veteran calm down, and arranges for follow-up care with mental health professionals. Her timely intervention helps the veteran feel supported and safe during a critical moment.

# The Impact of Providing Hope and Comfort

## *Enhanced Emotional Resilience*

Coping with Challenges

The hope and comfort provided by chaplains help veterans and their families develop the emotional resilience needed to cope with ongoing challenges. This resilience enables them to face difficulties with greater strength and confidence.

Reducing Stress and Anxiety

Spiritual practices, emotional support, and practical assistance significantly reduce stress and anxiety. Veterans and their families experience improved mental health and a greater sense of peace, contributing to overall well-being.

## *Strengthened Spiritual Well-Being*

Deepening Faith

The spiritual guidance offered by chaplains helps veterans and their families deepen their faith. This spiritual growth provides a strong foundation for navigating life's challenges and finding meaning and purpose.

Engagement in faith-based community programs and support groups fosters a sense of belonging and connection. These relationships provide ongoing support, encouragement, and companionship, enhancing spiritual well-being and quality of life.

# Case Study: Providing Hope and Comfort

## *Background*

### Veteran Profile

Mark, a Gulf War veteran, struggled with chronic pain and PTSD. His condition affected his daily life and strained his relationships with his family. Mark felt hopeless and disconnected from his faith.

## *Chaplain's Approach*

### Initial Assessment

Chaplain James conducted a comprehensive assessment to understand Mark's spiritual, emotional, and practical needs. He learned about Mark's background, current struggles, and spiritual beliefs.

### Developing a Care Plan

Based on the assessment, James developed a holistic care plan that included one-on-one counseling, participation in a support group, and engagement in faith-based activities.

## Providing Care

### Spiritual Guidance

James met with Mark regularly for counseling sessions, providing spiritual guidance and emotional support. They prayed together, discussed scriptures, and explored ways to reconnect with Mark's faith.

### Support Group

James encouraged Mark to join a PTSD support group. The group offered Mark a sense of community and mutual understanding, helping him feel less isolated and more supported.

### Faith-Based Activities

Mark began attending weekly worship services and Bible study sessions organized by James. These activities helped Mark find spiritual nourishment and a renewed sense of hope.

## Outcome

### Improved Emotional Well-Being

Through the support of James and the community, Mark's emotional well-being significantly improved. His PTSD symptoms became more manageable, and his relationships with his family strengthened.



Mark's engagement in faith-based activities helped him reconnect with his faith and find a renewed sense of purpose. He became more involved in his church and started volunteering, using his experiences to help other veterans.

# Conclusion

Providing hope and comfort is a central aspect of VA Chaplaincy. Through spiritual guidance, emotional support, community engagement, and practical assistance, chaplains help veterans and their families navigate difficult times. The impact of these efforts is profound, enhancing emotional resilience, strengthening spiritual well-being, and improving overall quality of life. The following chapters will continue to explore the various aspects of VA Chaplaincy, highlighting the essential role of chaplains in supporting and healing the veteran community.

## END-OF-LIFE CARE

# Introduction

End-of-life care is a profoundly important aspect of VA Chaplaincy, where the focus shifts to providing comfort, dignity, and spiritual support to terminally ill veterans and their families. VA Chaplains play a crucial role in this sensitive phase, offering emotional and spiritual guidance, facilitating meaningful rituals, and ensuring that veterans' final days are marked by peace and respect. This chapter explores the various facets of end-of-life care provided by VA Chaplains, highlighting their compassionate and essential contributions.

# The Role of VA Chaplains in End-of-Life Care

## *Providing Emotional and Spiritual Support*

### Emotional Presence

One of the most critical roles of VA Chaplains in end-of-life care is simply being present. This presence provides a calming and comforting influence, helping veterans and their families navigate the emotional complexities of impending death.

### *Example: Companion Visits*

Chaplain Maria spends time with terminally ill veterans, offering companionship and a listening ear. Her presence provides comfort and allows veterans to express their fears, hopes, and reflections, easing their emotional burden.

### Spiritual Guidance

Chaplains offer spiritual guidance tailored to the beliefs and needs of the veteran. This can include prayer, scripture reading, and discussions about faith, the afterlife, and finding peace in their final days.

Chaplain David meets regularly with veterans to discuss their spiritual concerns and provide reassurance. These conversations help veterans find solace and strength in their faith, bringing a sense of peace and acceptance.

## Facilitating Meaningful Rituals

Religious Rites

Conducting religious rites and rituals is a fundamental aspect of end-of-life care. These practices provide spiritual comfort, help veterans feel connected to their faith, and offer a sense of closure.

*Example: Last Rites and Communion*

Chaplain Sarah administers last rites and communion to terminally ill veterans who request these sacraments. These rituals provide profound spiritual comfort, reinforcing the veterans' faith and preparing them for their final journey.

Memorial Services

Chaplains help plan and conduct memorial services and funerals, ensuring that these ceremonies honor the veteran's life and service. These services provide families with a sense of closure and a way to celebrate their loved one's legacy.

*Example: Personalized Memorial Services*

Chaplain James collaborates with families to create personalized memorial services that reflect the veteran's faith, values, and life story. These services are deeply meaningful and provide a space for loved ones to grieve and celebrate the veteran's life.

## Supporting Families

Counseling and Emotional Support

Chaplains offer counseling and emotional support to families of terminally ill veterans. They help families process their grief, navigate complex emotions, and prepare for the impending loss.

*Example: Family Counseling Sessions*

Chaplain Maria holds counseling sessions with families, providing a safe space for them to express their feelings and find mutual support. Her guidance helps families cope with their grief and strengthens their emotional resilience.

Providing Resources

Chaplains connect families with resources such as grief support groups, bereavement counseling, and other services offered by the VA. These resources provide ongoing support to families before and after the veteran's passing.

*Example: Resource Coordination*

Chaplain David ensures that families have access to necessary resources, such as hospice care and bereavement services. This support helps families manage practical concerns and find continued support in their grieving process.

# Integrating Palliative Care

## Holistic Approach

### Physical Comfort

Chaplains work closely with medical teams to ensure that veterans receive comprehensive palliative care. This holistic approach addresses physical comfort, pain management, and overall quality of life.

*Example: Coordinating with Medical Teams*

Chaplain Sarah collaborates with doctors and nurses to ensure that veterans' physical comfort is prioritized. Her involvement ensures that spiritual care complements medical treatment, providing holistic support.

### Emotional and Spiritual Care

Palliative care includes emotional and spiritual support, which are essential components of holistic care. Chaplains address the emotional and spiritual needs of veterans, enhancing their overall well-being.

*Example: Integrative Care Plans*

Chaplain James develops integrative care plans that include spiritual counseling, emotional support, and coordination with palliative care providers. These plans ensure that all aspects of the veteran's well-being are addressed.

# The Impact of End-of-Life Care

## *Providing Peace and Dignity*

Ensuring Dignity

Chaplains ensure that veterans experience dignity in their final days. This includes respecting their wishes, honoring their faith, and providing compassionate care.

*Example: Respecting Wishes*

Chaplain Maria ensures that veterans' end-of-life wishes are respected, whether related to specific rituals, family presence, or other personal preferences. This respect for their wishes reinforces their dignity and comfort.

Bringing Peace

The spiritual and emotional support provided by chaplains brings peace to terminally ill veterans. This peace helps them face their final days with acceptance and serenity.

*Example: Facilitating Peaceful Transitions*

Chaplain David facilitates peaceful transitions by providing continuous spiritual support and ensuring that veterans feel connected to their faith. This support helps veterans find inner peace and face the end of life with tranquility.

## *Supporting Grieving Families*

Chaplains offer comfort and reassurance to grieving families, helping them navigate their loss and find strength in their faith and community.

*Example: Ongoing Family Support*

Chaplain Sarah provides ongoing support to families after the veteran's passing, offering counseling, prayer, and access to bereavement resources. Her continued presence helps families find comfort and healing.

Creating Lasting Memories

By facilitating meaningful rituals and memorial services, chaplains help families create lasting memories of their loved ones. These memories provide comfort and a way to honor the veteran's legacy.

*Example: Memorial Services*

Chaplain James helps families plan and conduct memorial services that celebrate the veteran's life and service. These services provide a space for families to grieve, remember, and celebrate their loved one's life.

# Case Study: Providing End-of-Life Care

*Background*

Veteran Profile

Jane, a Vietnam War veteran, was diagnosed with terminal cancer. She struggled with pain, fear of death, and concern for her family's well-being after her passing.

## Chaplain's Approach

Initial Assessment

Chaplain Maria conducted a comprehensive assessment to understand Jane's spiritual, emotional, and practical needs. She learned about Jane's faith background, her fears, and her end-of-life wishes.

Developing a Care Plan

Based on the assessment, Maria developed a holistic care plan that included spiritual counseling, pain management coordination, and family support.

## Providing Care

Spiritual and Emotional Support

Maria provided regular spiritual counseling and emotional support to Jane. They prayed together, discussed scriptures, and explored Jane's feelings about death and the afterlife. Maria's support helped Jane find peace and acceptance.

Family Support

Maria offered counseling and practical assistance to Jane's family, helping them prepare for her passing and navigate their grief. She connected them with hospice care and bereavement services.

Facilitating Rituals

Maria conducted last rites and organized a memorial service that reflected Jane's faith and life. These rituals provided Jane and her family with spiritual comfort and a sense of closure.

## *Outcome*

Peaceful Passing

With Maria's support, Jane experienced a peaceful and dignified passing. She felt connected to her faith and reassured about her family's well-being.

Comforted Family

Jane's family found comfort in Maria's guidance and the meaningful rituals she facilitated. The memorial service provided them with a way to honor Jane's life and find solace in their grief.

# Conclusion

End-of-life care is a profoundly important aspect of VA Chaplaincy. VA Chaplains provide terminally ill veterans and their families with emotional and spiritual support, facilitate meaningful rituals, and ensure that veterans experience dignity and peace in their final days. Through their compassionate and holistic approach, chaplains make a significant impact on the lives of veterans and their families, helping them navigate the difficult journey of end-of-life care with comfort and hope. The following chapters will continue to explore the various aspects of VA Chaplaincy, highlighting the essential role of chaplains in supporting and healing the veteran community.

# CHAPTER 07

---

## FAITH AND GUIDANCE IN VA CHAPLAINCY

## SPIRITUAL GUIDANCE

# Introduction

VA Chaplains play a vital role in providing spiritual guidance to veterans from diverse faith backgrounds. This guidance is essential for helping veterans navigate their spiritual journeys, find meaning and purpose, and cope with the challenges they face. VA Chaplains offer individualized support, respect different beliefs, and employ a variety of practices to meet the unique needs of each veteran. This chapter explores how VA Chaplains provide spiritual guidance to veterans of various faiths and beliefs.

# The Diversity of Faiths Among Veterans

*Recognizing Diversity*

## Varied Beliefs

Veterans come from a wide array of religious and spiritual backgrounds, including Christianity, Islam, Judaism, Buddhism, Hinduism, and secular or non-religious perspectives. Recognizing and respecting this diversity is crucial for effective spiritual guidance.

## Inclusive Approach

VA Chaplains adopt an inclusive approach, ensuring that all veterans feel respected and supported regardless of their faith or belief system. This inclusivity fosters a welcoming environment where veterans can explore and express their spirituality freely.

# Providing Individualized Spiritual Guidance

## *Spiritual Assessments*

### Understanding Needs

Chaplains conduct spiritual assessments to understand the unique spiritual needs, beliefs, and practices of each veteran. These assessments involve conversations about the veteran's faith background, current spiritual practices, and any specific concerns or questions they may have.

### *Example: Comprehensive Assessments*

Chaplain Sarah conducts thorough spiritual assessments during her initial meetings with veterans. She asks open-ended questions about their faith journey, spiritual practices, and current challenges. This information helps her tailor her guidance to each veteran's specific needs.



Based on the spiritual assessment, chaplains develop personalized spiritual care plans. These plans outline the types of support and practices that will best meet the veteran's needs and help them achieve their spiritual goals.

*Example: Tailored Care Plans*

Chaplain David creates personalized care plans for each veteran he supports. These plans include regular meetings for spiritual counseling, participation in relevant faith-based activities, and specific practices such as prayer, meditation, or scripture reading.

## Offering Spiritual Counseling

One-on-One Sessions

Chaplains provide one-on-one spiritual counseling sessions where veterans can discuss their spiritual concerns, explore their beliefs, and seek guidance. These sessions offer a confidential and supportive space for veterans to delve into their spirituality.

*Example: Personal Counseling*

Chaplain Maria meets regularly with veterans for spiritual counseling. In these sessions, she listens attentively to their concerns, offers insights from their faith traditions, and helps them find spiritual solutions to their challenges.

## Addressing Specific Issues

Spiritual counseling often involves addressing specific issues such as moral injury, guilt, grief, and existential questions. Chaplains use their knowledge of various faith traditions to provide relevant and meaningful guidance.

*Example: Addressing Moral Injury*

Chaplain James works with veterans dealing with moral injury. He helps them explore concepts of forgiveness, redemption, and reconciliation within their faith traditions, providing a path to spiritual healing and peace.

# Facilitating Spiritual Practices

## *Leading Prayer and Meditation*

### Guided Practices

Chaplains lead veterans in guided spiritual practices such as prayer and meditation. These practices provide a sense of peace, connection, and spiritual nourishment, helping veterans cope with stress and find inner calm.

*Example: Meditation Sessions*

Chaplain Sarah leads mindfulness meditation sessions for veterans. These sessions include guided breathing exercises and meditations focused on cultivating peace and presence. Veterans find these practices helpful in managing anxiety and enhancing spiritual well-being.

Spiritual practices can be conducted individually or in group settings, depending on the veteran's preferences and needs. Group sessions offer a sense of community and shared experience, while individual sessions provide personalized attention.

*Example: Group Prayer*

Chaplain David organizes group prayer sessions where veterans can come together to pray, share their intentions, and support one another spiritually. These sessions foster a sense of community and mutual encouragement.

## Conducting Religious Services

Inclusive Worship

Chaplains conduct religious services that are inclusive and respectful of diverse beliefs. These services provide veterans with opportunities to engage in worship, reflect on their faith, and connect with a spiritual community.

*Example: Interfaith Services*

Chaplain Maria organizes interfaith services that include prayers, readings, and reflections from various religious traditions. These services create an inclusive space where veterans of different faiths can come together in worship and mutual respect.

Celebrating Religious Holidays

Chaplains help veterans celebrate religious holidays and observances, providing opportunities for spiritual reflection and community engagement. These celebrations honor the veterans' faith traditions and enhance their spiritual well-being.

*Example: Holiday Celebrations*

Chaplain James organizes celebrations for major religious holidays, such as Christmas, Hanukkah, Ramadan, and Diwali. These events include worship services, festive meals, and community activities, helping veterans feel connected to their faith and community.

# Respecting and Honoring Different Beliefs

## *Interfaith Understanding*

Cultural Competence

Chaplains strive to develop cultural competence and interfaith understanding. This involves learning about different religious traditions, practices, and beliefs, and being sensitive to the unique needs of veterans from diverse backgrounds.

*Example: Continuous Learning*

Chaplain Sarah participates in workshops and training sessions on cultural competence and interfaith understanding. This ongoing education helps her provide respectful and informed spiritual guidance to veterans of various faiths.

Building strong relationships with veterans from different faith backgrounds is essential for effective spiritual guidance. Chaplains show respect, empathy, and openness, fostering trust and mutual respect.

*Example: Interfaith Dialogues*

Chaplain David facilitates interfaith dialogues where veterans can share their beliefs and learn about other traditions. These dialogues promote understanding and respect, enhancing the spiritual community within the VA.

## *Providing Resources*

Access to Faith-Specific Materials

Chaplains ensure that veterans have access to faith-specific materials such as religious texts, prayer books, and other spiritual resources. These materials support veterans in their spiritual practices and provide comfort and guidance.

*Example: Resource Library*

Chaplain Maria maintains a resource library with religious texts, prayer books, and spiritual literature from various faith traditions. Veterans can borrow these materials to support their spiritual journey and deepen their understanding of their faith.

Connecting with Faith Communities

Chaplains help veterans connect with local faith communities and religious leaders. These connections provide additional spiritual support and resources, enhancing the veterans' spiritual lives.

*Example: Community Partnerships*

Chaplain James builds partnerships with local churches, mosques, synagogues, and temples. He facilitates introductions and connections for veterans who wish to engage with these faith communities, providing them with broader spiritual support.

# Case Study: Spiritual Guidance in Action

## *Background*

Veteran Profile

Alex, a recently retired Marine, struggled with feelings of guilt and existential questions after his service. He identified as a Christian but had not been active in his faith for many years.

## *Chaplain's Approach*

Initial Assessment

Chaplain Sarah conducted a spiritual assessment to understand Alex's faith background, current spiritual concerns, and specific needs. She learned about his feelings of guilt and his desire to reconnect with his faith.

Developing a Care Plan

Based on the assessment, Sarah developed a personalized care plan that included regular spiritual counseling, participation in a Christian fellowship group, and engagement in prayer and scripture reading.

## *Providing Care*

Spiritual Counseling

Sarah met with Alex weekly for spiritual counseling sessions. They discussed his feelings of guilt, explored Christian teachings on forgiveness and redemption, and prayed together. These sessions helped Alex find peace and spiritual clarity.

Fellowship Group

Sarah encouraged Alex to join a Christian fellowship group within the VA. The group provided a supportive community where Alex could share his experiences, engage in Bible study, and participate in worship.

Personal Spiritual Practices

Sarah guided Alex in developing personal spiritual practices, such as daily prayer and scripture reading. These practices helped Alex reconnect with his faith and find spiritual strength.

## *Outcome*

Renewed Faith

Through Sarah's guidance, Alex experienced a renewal of his faith. He found forgiveness for his past actions and developed a deeper connection with his spiritual beliefs.

Improved Well-Being

Alex's emotional and spiritual well-being significantly improved. He felt more at peace, connected to a supportive community, and equipped with spiritual tools to navigate his post-service life.

# Conclusion

VA Chaplains provide essential spiritual guidance to veterans from diverse faith backgrounds. Through individualized support, inclusive practices, and a deep respect for different beliefs, chaplains help veterans navigate their spiritual journeys, find meaning and purpose, and cope with the challenges they face. The compassionate and tailored approach of VA Chaplains ensures that all veterans receive the spiritual care and support they need, enhancing their overall well-being and quality of life. The following chapters will continue to explore the various aspects of VA Chaplaincy, highlighting the profound impact of this crucial ministry on the veteran community.

## INTERFAITH MINISTRY

# Introduction

Interfaith ministry is a crucial aspect of VA Chaplaincy, given the diverse religious backgrounds of veterans. VA Chaplains must be equipped to provide spiritual support that respects and honors this diversity. Interfaith ministry involves understanding different faith traditions, fostering an inclusive environment, and building bridges between various religious communities. This chapter explores the importance of interfaith ministry in the VA and how chaplains navigate the challenges and opportunities it presents.

# The Importance of Interfaith Ministry

## Recognizing Diversity in Faith

### A Spectrum of Beliefs

Veterans come from a wide range of religious traditions, including Christianity, Islam, Judaism, Buddhism, Hinduism, and various indigenous and secular beliefs. Recognizing and respecting this diversity is essential for providing effective spiritual care.

### Inclusive Spiritual Support

Interfaith ministry ensures that all veterans receive spiritual support that aligns with their beliefs. This inclusivity fosters a sense of belonging and respect, enhancing the overall well-being of veterans.

## Promoting Understanding and Respect

Fostering Mutual Respect

Interfaith ministry promotes mutual respect among veterans from different religious backgrounds. By creating an environment where diverse beliefs are honored, chaplains help reduce prejudice and foster a culture of respect and understanding.

Enhancing Community Cohesion

An inclusive approach to spiritual care helps build a cohesive community within the VA. Veterans from different faith traditions can come together, share their experiences, and support one another, strengthening the overall sense of community.

# Practices of Interfaith Ministry

## *Education and Training*

Cultural Competence

VA Chaplains undergo training in cultural competence and interfaith understanding. This education helps them understand the nuances of different religious traditions and how to provide respectful and informed spiritual care.

*Example: Training Programs*

Chaplain Maria participates in regular training programs on cultural competence and interfaith ministry. These programs enhance her understanding of various faith traditions and improve her ability to provide inclusive spiritual support.

Continuous Learning

Interfaith ministry requires continuous learning and openness to new perspectives. Chaplains stay informed about developments in various religious traditions and seek opportunities to deepen their understanding.

*Example: Interfaith Dialogues*

Chaplain David attends interfaith dialogues and workshops, where he learns from religious leaders and scholars about different faith traditions. This ongoing education helps him stay current and informed.

## Building Relationships

Engaging with Faith Communities

Chaplains build relationships with local faith communities and religious leaders. These connections provide additional resources and support for veterans and enhance the chaplain's ability to provide informed spiritual care.

*Example: Community Partnerships*

Chaplain Sarah establishes partnerships with local churches, mosques, synagogues, and temples. These partnerships facilitate referrals, collaborative events, and mutual support between the VA and local faith communities.

Creating Inclusive Spaces

Chaplains create inclusive spaces within the VA where veterans from different faith traditions can gather, worship, and support one another. These spaces foster a sense of belonging and respect.

*Example: Interfaith Chapel*

Chaplain James oversees an interfaith chapel at the VA facility. The chapel is designed to accommodate various religious practices and serves as a welcoming space for veterans of all faiths.

## Providing Spiritual Support

Tailored Spiritual Care

Chaplains provide spiritual care tailored to the specific beliefs and practices of each veteran. This individualized approach ensures that veterans receive support that aligns with their faith.

*Example: Personalized Support*

Chaplain Maria conducts spiritual assessments to understand each veteran's faith background and spiritual needs. She then tailors her support to align with their beliefs, offering personalized spiritual care.

Facilitating Interfaith Activities

Chaplains organize interfaith activities that bring veterans from different religious backgrounds together. These activities promote understanding, respect, and a sense of community.

Chaplain David organizes interfaith prayer services that include readings, prayers, and reflections from various religious traditions. These services foster a spirit of inclusivity and mutual respect.

# Challenges and Opportunities in Interfaith Ministry

## *Navigating Religious Differences*

### Respecting Diverse Beliefs

One of the challenges of interfaith ministry is respecting diverse beliefs while providing meaningful spiritual care. Chaplains must navigate these differences with sensitivity and respect.

*Example: Respectful Dialogue*

Chaplain Sarah engages in respectful dialogue with veterans about their beliefs. She listens attentively and honors their perspectives, ensuring that her support is respectful and inclusive.

### Addressing Conflicts

Conflicts may arise when veterans' beliefs and practices differ significantly. Chaplains play a crucial role in mediating these conflicts and promoting a culture of respect and understanding.

*Example: Conflict Resolution*

Chaplain James mediates conflicts that arise due to religious differences. He facilitates conversations that promote mutual understanding and respect, helping veterans find common ground.

## Leveraging Opportunities for Growth

### Enhancing Cultural Competence

Interfaith ministry offers opportunities for chaplains to enhance their cultural competence and deepen their understanding of various religious traditions.

*Example: Learning from Peers*

Chaplain Maria learns from her peers in interfaith ministry, gaining insights into different religious practices and perspectives. This collaborative learning enhances her ability to provide inclusive spiritual care.

### Building a Diverse Community

Interfaith activities and inclusive practices help build a diverse and supportive community within the VA. This diversity enriches the spiritual lives of veterans and fosters a culture of mutual respect.

*Example: Community Building*

Chaplain David organizes community-building activities that celebrate the diversity of faiths within the VA. These activities include cultural festivals, interfaith dialogues, and collaborative service projects.

# Case Study: Successful Interfaith Ministry

## *Background*

Veteran Profile

Ahmed, a Muslim veteran, sought spiritual support after experiencing prejudice and isolation within the VA. He wanted to connect with other veterans and find a supportive community that respected his faith.

## *Chaplain's Approach*

Initial Assessment

Chaplain Sarah conducted a spiritual assessment to understand Ahmed's experiences, beliefs, and needs. She learned about his desire for community and his struggles with prejudice.

Developing a Care Plan

Based on the assessment, Sarah developed a care plan that included individual spiritual counseling, participation in interfaith activities, and connection with the local Muslim community.

## *Providing Care*

Spiritual Counseling

Sarah provided regular spiritual counseling to Ahmed, offering support and guidance aligned with his Islamic beliefs. These sessions helped Ahmed navigate his spiritual journey and cope with his challenges.

Interfaith Activities

Sarah encouraged Ahmed to participate in interfaith activities at the VA. These activities included interfaith prayer services, cultural festivals, and dialogues that promoted mutual understanding and respect.

Community Connection

Sarah facilitated Ahmed's connection with the local Muslim community, introducing him to a nearby mosque and its leaders. This connection provided Ahmed with additional spiritual support and a sense of belonging.

## *Outcome*

Enhanced Well-Being

Through Sarah's support, Ahmed experienced significant improvements in his well-being. He felt more connected to his faith, supported by his community, and respected within the VA.

Strengthened Community

Ahmed's participation in interfaith activities helped strengthen the community within the VA. His experiences and contributions enriched the interfaith dialogue and fostered mutual respect among veterans.

# Conclusion

Interfaith ministry is a vital aspect of VA Chaplaincy, providing essential spiritual support to veterans from diverse religious backgrounds. Through education, relationship-building, and inclusive practices, chaplains navigate the challenges and opportunities of interfaith ministry. Their efforts foster a culture of respect, understanding, and mutual support, enhancing the spiritual and emotional well-being of all veterans. The following chapters will continue to explore the various aspects of VA Chaplaincy, highlighting the profound impact of this crucial ministry on the veteran community.

## ETHICAL CONSIDERATIONS

# Introduction

VA Chaplains face numerous ethical considerations as they provide spiritual care to veterans from diverse backgrounds. These considerations include maintaining confidentiality, respecting different belief systems, navigating dual relationships, and upholding professional boundaries. Ethical behavior is fundamental to building trust and providing effective support. This chapter examines the key ethical considerations VA Chaplains must navigate and the principles that guide their practice.

# Maintaining Confidentiality

## Importance of Confidentiality

### Building Trust

Confidentiality is essential for building trust between chaplains and veterans. Veterans need to feel confident that their personal and spiritual concerns will be kept private to open up and share honestly.

### Ethical Obligation

Maintaining confidentiality is an ethical obligation and a professional standard in chaplaincy. It ensures that veterans' privacy is respected and their sensitive information is protected.

## Navigating Confidentiality

### Confidential Discussions

Chaplains must ensure that all discussions with veterans are confidential unless the veteran gives explicit consent to share information. This includes private counseling sessions and spiritual assessments.

*Example: Private Counseling*

Chaplain Sarah assures veterans that their conversations will remain confidential. She explains the boundaries of confidentiality and reassures them that their privacy will be respected.

There are specific situations where confidentiality may need to be breached, such as when there is a risk of harm to the veteran or others. In these cases, chaplains must navigate the ethical dilemma of protecting confidentiality while ensuring safety.

*Example: Risk of Harm*

Chaplain James encounters a veteran expressing suicidal thoughts. He explains that while confidentiality is important, he must report this information to ensure the veteran's safety. He works with mental health professionals to provide the necessary support while maintaining as much privacy as possible.

# Respecting Different Belief Systems

## *Inclusivity and Respect*

### Honoring Diversity

VA Chaplains must honor the diversity of beliefs among veterans. This involves respecting different religious traditions, spiritual practices, and worldviews, and providing care that aligns with each veteran's beliefs.

### Avoiding Imposition

Chaplains must avoid imposing their beliefs on veterans. Their role is to support and guide veterans in their spiritual journey, not to convert or persuade them to adopt a particular faith.

## *Navigating Religious Differences*

### Cultural Competence

Chaplains develop cultural competence by learning about different religious traditions and practices. This knowledge helps them provide respectful and informed spiritual care.

*Example: Learning About Different Faiths*

Chaplain Maria continuously educates herself about various faith traditions, including attending interfaith workshops and reading religious texts. This ongoing learning helps her support veterans from diverse backgrounds.

### Facilitating Interfaith Activities

Chaplains facilitate interfaith activities that promote understanding and respect among veterans of different beliefs. These activities help build a cohesive and inclusive community within the VA.

*Example: Interfaith Dialogues*

Chaplain David organizes interfaith dialogues where veterans can share their beliefs and learn about other traditions. These dialogues foster mutual respect and understanding, enhancing the spiritual community.

# Navigating Dual Relationships

## *Understanding Dual Relationships*

Professional Boundaries

Dual relationships occur when chaplains have multiple roles with a veteran, such as being both a spiritual advisor and a friend. These relationships can complicate professional boundaries and ethical obligations.

Potential Conflicts

Dual relationships can lead to conflicts of interest and challenges in maintaining objectivity. Chaplains must be mindful of these potential conflicts and manage their relationships accordingly.

## *Managing Dual Relationships*

Establishing Clear Boundaries

Chaplains establish clear boundaries to navigate dual relationships ethically. They communicate their professional role and the limits of their relationship with veterans.

*Example: Setting Boundaries*

Chaplain Sarah explains to veterans that while she is there to support them spiritually, their relationship must remain professional to ensure effective and unbiased care. She sets boundaries to avoid conflicts of interest.

Seeking Supervision and Guidance

Chaplains seek supervision and guidance when navigating dual relationships. Consulting with colleagues or supervisors helps them manage these relationships ethically and effectively.

*Example: Supervision Sessions*

Chaplain James regularly attends supervision sessions where he discusses challenging dual relationships with his supervisor. These sessions provide him with guidance and support in maintaining professional boundaries.

# Upholding Professional Boundaries

## *Importance of Boundaries*

Ensuring Ethical Practice

Professional boundaries ensure that chaplains practice ethically and maintain the integrity of their role. Boundaries protect both the chaplain and the veteran from potential harm and conflicts of interest.

Enhancing Trust

Clear professional boundaries enhance trust between chaplains and veterans. Veterans need to feel confident that their chaplain is acting in their best interest and maintaining ethical standards.

## *Navigating Professional Boundaries*

Avoiding Exploitation

Chaplains must avoid exploiting their relationship with veterans for personal gain. This includes refraining from any behavior that could be perceived as taking advantage of the veteran's vulnerability.

*Example: Ethical Behavior*

Chaplain Maria ensures that her interactions with veterans are always professional and focused on their needs. She avoids any behavior that could be seen as exploitative or self-serving.

Maintaining Objectivity

Chaplains maintain objectivity in their interactions with veterans. This involves providing unbiased support and avoiding favoritism or preferential treatment.

*Example: Unbiased Support*

Chaplain David treats all veterans with the same level of care and respect, regardless of their background or beliefs. He ensures that his support is unbiased and focused on the veterans' well-being.

# Case Study: Navigating Ethical Considerations

*Background*

Veteran Profile

John, a veteran struggling with PTSD, sought spiritual support from Chaplain Sarah. He shared deeply personal experiences and relied on her for emotional and spiritual guidance.

## Ethical Considerations

Confidentiality

Sarah assured John that their conversations would remain confidential, explaining the boundaries of confidentiality and the exceptions in case of risk to his safety.

Respecting Beliefs

John identified as a Buddhist, and Sarah respected his beliefs by incorporating Buddhist practices and teachings into their sessions. She avoided imposing her beliefs and focused on supporting his spiritual journey.

Professional Boundaries

Sarah maintained professional boundaries by clearly defining her role and the limits of their relationship. She sought supervision to ensure she managed the relationship ethically.

## Outcome

Trust and Support

Through Sarah's ethical practice, John felt supported and respected. He trusted Sarah with his personal experiences and found spiritual guidance that aligned with his beliefs.

John's emotional and spiritual well-being improved as a result of the ethical and respectful care he received. He felt more at peace and better equipped to manage his PTSD.

# Conclusion

Navigating ethical considerations is fundamental to the practice of VA Chaplains. By maintaining confidentiality, respecting diverse beliefs, managing dual relationships, and upholding professional boundaries, chaplains provide effective and ethical spiritual care. These ethical principles ensure that veterans receive respectful, unbiased, and supportive guidance, enhancing their overall well-being. The following chapters will continue to explore the various aspects of VA Chaplaincy, highlighting the profound impact of this crucial ministry on the veteran community.

# CHAPTER 08

---

**REFLECTING ON THE JOURNEY**

**REFLECTING ON THE JOURNEY**

## Introduction

As we conclude this exploration of the role of VA Chaplains, it is essential to reflect on the profound impact these dedicated individuals have on the lives of veterans. Throughout this book, we have examined various aspects of VA Chaplaincy, from providing spiritual guidance and emotional support to navigating ethical considerations and fostering a sense of community. This chapter summarizes the key points discussed and highlights the significant contributions of VA Chaplains to the well-being and healing of veterans.

## Summary of Key Points

## *The Role of VA Chaplains*

### Spiritual Guidance

VA Chaplains provide essential spiritual guidance to veterans, helping them navigate their faith journeys, find meaning, and cope with life's challenges. Through personalized counseling, prayer, and spiritual practices, chaplains support veterans in deepening their faith and finding inner peace.

### Emotional Support

Chaplains offer emotional support to veterans dealing with various issues, including PTSD, grief, moral injury, and depression. Their compassionate presence and active listening provide veterans with a safe space to express their feelings and find healing.

### Practical Assistance

VA Chaplains assist veterans in accessing resources, navigating the VA system, and connecting with community support. This practical assistance helps veterans manage the complexities of their lives and enhances their overall well-being.

## *Specialized Care*

### End-of-Life Care

Chaplains provide compassionate end-of-life care, ensuring that terminally ill veterans experience dignity, peace, and spiritual comfort in their final days. They support both veterans and their families, offering guidance and facilitating meaningful rituals.

### Interfaith Ministry

Recognizing the diverse religious backgrounds of veterans, chaplains engage in interfaith ministry. They respect and honor different belief systems, fostering an inclusive environment and promoting mutual respect and understanding.

### Ethical Considerations

VA Chaplains navigate complex ethical considerations, including maintaining confidentiality, respecting diverse beliefs, and upholding professional boundaries. Their commitment to ethical practice ensures that veterans receive respectful and unbiased care.

## *Community and Connection*

### Building Community

Chaplains play a vital role in building a sense of community among veterans. Through support groups, faith-based programs, and interfaith activities, they foster connections and create a supportive environment where veterans can share their experiences and support one another.

### Providing Hope and Comfort

Chaplains provide hope and comfort to veterans and their families during difficult times. Their spiritual guidance, emotional support, and practical assistance help veterans find strength, resilience, and peace.

# The Profound Impact of VA Chaplains

## *Healing and Transformation*

### Spiritual Renewal

Through their guidance and support, VA Chaplains help veterans experience spiritual renewal. This renewal provides veterans with a sense of purpose, inner peace, and a deeper connection to their faith.

*Example: John's Spiritual Journey*

John, a veteran struggling with PTSD, found spiritual renewal through the guidance of Chaplain David. Through regular counseling and participation in faith-based activities, John deepened his faith and found peace, transforming his outlook on life.

### Emotional Resilience

Chaplains help veterans build emotional resilience, equipping them with coping strategies and emotional support to face life's challenges. This resilience enhances their overall well-being and quality of life.

*Example: Maria's Resilience*

Maria, a grieving widow, found emotional resilience through the support of Chaplain Sarah. Through grief counseling and community support, Maria navigated her grief and emerged stronger, finding new meaning and purpose in her life.

## *Strengthening Families and Communities*

Family Support

Chaplains provide essential support to the families of veterans, helping them navigate complex emotions and challenges. This support strengthens family bonds and enhances the well-being of both veterans and their loved ones.

*Example: The Smith Family*

The Smith family received comprehensive support from Chaplain James during a difficult time. His guidance and compassionate care helped them cope with their grief and rebuild their relationships, fostering a stronger and more supportive family dynamic.

Building Inclusive Communities

Through interfaith activities and inclusive practices, chaplains build diverse and supportive communities within the VA. These communities foster mutual respect, understanding, and a sense of belonging among veterans from various backgrounds.

*Example: Interfaith Community*

Chaplain Maria's efforts in building an interfaith community at the VA created a welcoming and inclusive environment. Veterans from different faith traditions came together, shared their experiences, and supported one another, enriching the spiritual community.

# Final Reflections

## The Essential Role of VA Chaplains

### Dedicated Service

VA Chaplains are dedicated to serving veterans with compassion, respect, and integrity. Their unwavering commitment to providing spiritual and emotional care makes a significant difference in the lives of those they serve.

### Lasting Impact

The impact of VA Chaplains extends beyond individual veterans. Their work strengthens families, builds communities, and fosters a culture of respect and understanding. The positive effects of their ministry are profound and long-lasting.

## Looking Ahead

### Continuing the Mission

As the needs of veterans evolve, VA Chaplains will continue to adapt and expand their services. Their mission remains the same: to provide compassionate and inclusive spiritual care that supports the well-being and healing of veterans.

### Embracing Diversity

The diversity of the veteran population is a strength that VA Chaplains will continue to embrace. By honoring different beliefs and fostering inclusivity, chaplains will build stronger and more supportive communities within the VA.

# Conclusion

Reflecting on the journey of VA Chaplaincy reveals the profound and far-reaching impact of this vital ministry. VA Chaplains provide essential spiritual guidance, emotional support, and practical assistance, helping veterans navigate their unique challenges and find healing and hope. Their dedication, compassion, and ethical practice enrich the lives of veterans and their families, fostering a culture of respect, understanding, and community. As we look to the future, the continued mission of VA Chaplains remains a cornerstone of support for the veteran community, ensuring that all veterans receive the care and respect they deserve.

## THE FUTURE OF VA CHAPLAINCY

# Introduction

As we reflect on the significant impact of VA Chaplaincy on the lives of veterans, it is also essential to consider the future of this vital ministry. The landscape of veterans' affairs continues to evolve, and so too must the role of VA Chaplains. This chapter explores the ongoing need for spiritual support in veterans' affairs and the future directions of VA Chaplaincy, emphasizing the importance of adaptability, innovation, and a continued commitment to compassionate care.

# The Ongoing Need for Spiritual Support

*Evolving Challenges for Veterans*

The demographics of the veteran population are changing, with increasing numbers of women, minorities, and younger veterans from recent conflicts. This diversity brings new challenges and requires chaplains to adapt their services to meet the needs of all veterans effectively.



New issues such as cybersecurity threats, the psychological impact of drone warfare, and the effects of prolonged deployments are emerging. These challenges necessitate updated approaches to spiritual care and support.

## *The Role of Spiritual Care*



Spiritual care remains a crucial component of holistic healing. Addressing the spiritual needs of veterans complements physical and mental health treatments, fostering overall well-being and resilience.



Veterans often face complex moral and ethical dilemmas stemming from their service. VA Chaplains provide essential guidance, helping veterans reconcile their actions with their values and beliefs, and find peace and redemption.

# Future Directions for VA Chaplaincy

## Embracing Technology

Telechaplaincy

The use of technology in providing spiritual care, such as telechaplaincy, has become increasingly important, especially in the wake of the COVID-19 pandemic. Telechaplaincy allows chaplains to reach veterans who may be geographically isolated or unable to visit VA facilities in person.

*Example: Virtual Counseling Sessions*

Chaplain Sarah offers virtual counseling sessions to veterans in remote areas. This approach ensures that all veterans have access to spiritual support, regardless of their location.

Online Resources

Developing and providing access to online spiritual resources, such as guided meditations, prayer groups, and religious education materials, can enhance the reach and effectiveness of VA Chaplaincy.

*Example: Online Faith Community*

Chaplain David creates an online faith community where veterans can participate in virtual worship services, engage in faith-based discussions, and access spiritual resources. This platform fosters connection and support in a digital space.

## Expanding Interdisciplinary Collaboration

Integrated Care Teams

VA Chaplains will continue to play a vital role in integrated care teams, collaborating with medical professionals, mental health counselors, and social workers to provide comprehensive care. This interdisciplinary approach ensures that all aspects of a veteran's well-being are addressed.

*Example: Holistic Care Plans*

Chaplain Maria works closely with healthcare providers to develop holistic care plans for veterans. These plans include medical treatment, mental health support, and spiritual care, ensuring a comprehensive approach to healing.

Research and Best Practices

Engaging in research and sharing best practices within the field of chaplaincy and beyond can enhance the effectiveness of spiritual care. Chaplains can contribute to studies on the impact of spiritual care and develop evidence-based practices.

*Example: Collaborative Research*

Chaplain James collaborates with researchers to study the impact of spiritual care on PTSD symptoms. The findings help improve chaplaincy practices and demonstrate the value of spiritual support in veterans' care.

## Fostering Inclusivity and Diversity

Cultural Competence Training

Ongoing cultural competence training is essential for chaplains to effectively serve an increasingly diverse veteran population. This training ensures that chaplains are aware of and sensitive to the unique needs of veterans from various backgrounds.

*Example: Diversity Workshops*

Chaplain Sarah attends diversity workshops to enhance her understanding of different cultural and religious traditions. This training helps her provide inclusive and respectful spiritual care.

Inclusive Programs

Developing and implementing inclusive programs that honor the diverse beliefs and practices of veterans will be crucial. These programs foster a sense of belonging and respect within the VA community.

*Example: Multifaith Prayer Services*

Chaplain David organizes multifaith prayer services that include elements from various religious traditions. These services create a welcoming environment for all veterans, promoting mutual respect and understanding.

## Enhancing Support for Families

Recognizing the important role of families in veterans' lives, chaplains will continue to enhance their support for family members. Providing family-centered care ensures that the needs of both veterans and their loved ones are addressed.

*Example: Family Counseling*

Chaplain Maria offers family counseling sessions to help veterans and their families navigate challenges together. This support strengthens family bonds and enhances overall well-being.

Bereavement Support

Expanding bereavement support services for families who have lost a loved one ensures that they receive the care and guidance they need during difficult times.

*Example: Grief Support Groups*

Chaplain James facilitates grief support groups for families, providing a space for them to share their experiences, find comfort, and receive ongoing support.

# Conclusion

The future of VA Chaplaincy is marked by opportunities for growth, adaptation, and continued dedication to serving veterans and their families. As the needs of veterans evolve, so too will the approaches and practices of VA Chaplains. By embracing technology, expanding interdisciplinary collaboration, fostering inclusivity, and enhancing family support, VA Chaplains will continue to provide essential spiritual care that promotes healing, resilience, and well-being.

Reflecting on the journey of VA Chaplaincy underscores the profound impact that these dedicated individuals have on the lives of veterans. Their compassionate care, ethical practice, and unwavering commitment to supporting veterans through all stages of life ensure that the legacy of VA Chaplaincy will endure and thrive. As we look ahead, the mission of VA Chaplains remains clear: to provide holistic, inclusive, and compassionate spiritual care that honors the service and sacrifices of our veterans, ensuring they receive the respect and support they deserve.

# EPILOGUE



**A PERSON REFLECTION**

## MY JOURNEY AS A VA CHAPLAIN

As I reflect on my journey as a VA Chaplain, I am filled with a deep sense of gratitude and humility. This path has been both challenging and profoundly rewarding, shaping my understanding of faith, resilience, and the power of human connection. Through the years, I have had the honor of walking alongside veterans and their families, witnessing their struggles and triumphs, and offering support and guidance in their times of need. This epilogue is a personal reflection on my experiences and the lessons I have learned along the way.

## The Calling

My journey began with a calling—a profound sense of purpose that drew me to serve those who have served our country. From the outset, I was inspired by the courage and sacrifice of veterans, and I felt compelled to provide them with spiritual care and support. This calling was rooted in my faith and a deep belief in the importance of compassion and service.

# Early Experiences

## *Learning and Growth*

My early experiences as a VA Chaplain were marked by intense learning and growth. I encountered veterans from diverse backgrounds, each with their own unique stories and challenges. I learned to listen deeply, to offer empathy and understanding, and to adapt my approach to meet the specific needs of each individual. These early encounters taught me the importance of humility and the value of being fully present for those in need.

## *Building Trust*

Building trust with veterans was a fundamental aspect of my early work. Many veterans were initially hesitant to open up, having faced significant hardships and often feeling isolated or misunderstood. I learned that trust is earned through consistent, compassionate care and a genuine commitment to their well-being. Over time, I built strong relationships that became the foundation for meaningful spiritual guidance and support.

# Challenges and Triumphs

## *Navigating Ethical Dilemmas*

Throughout my journey, I have encountered numerous ethical dilemmas that required careful consideration and discernment. Maintaining confidentiality, respecting diverse belief systems, and managing dual relationships were just a few of the challenges I faced. Each situation reinforced the importance of ethical practice and the need to uphold the highest standards of integrity and respect.

## Witnessing Transformation

One of the most rewarding aspects of my journey has been witnessing the transformation in the lives of the veterans I have served. I have seen veterans find peace and healing through spiritual renewal, build resilience through emotional support, and reconnect with their faith and community. These moments of transformation are a testament to the power of compassionate care and the resilience of the human spirit.

# The Impact of Community

## Building Inclusive Spaces

Creating inclusive spaces where veterans from diverse backgrounds can come together and support one another has been a central focus of my work. I have facilitated interfaith activities, support groups, and community events that promote mutual respect and understanding. These inclusive spaces have fostered a sense of belonging and strengthened the overall VA community.

## Supporting Families

Supporting the families of veterans has been an integral part of my journey. I have provided counseling and guidance to families facing grief, stress, and uncertainty. Witnessing the strength and resilience of these families has been inspiring, and their stories have reinforced the importance of family-centered care.

# Looking Ahead

## *Embracing Change*

As I look to the future, I recognize the need to embrace change and adapt to the evolving needs of veterans. The use of technology, interdisciplinary collaboration, and ongoing cultural competence training will be essential in providing effective and inclusive care. I am committed to continuing my education and staying informed about new developments in chaplaincy and veterans' care.

## *Continuing the Mission*

The mission of VA Chaplaincy remains as vital as ever. As VA Chaplains, we are called to provide holistic, compassionate, and inclusive spiritual care that honors the service and sacrifices of our veterans. I am dedicated to continuing this mission, ensuring that every veteran receives the support and respect they deserve.

# Final Reflections

My journey as a VA Chaplain has been a profound and transformative experience. It has taught me the power of compassion, the importance of ethical practice, and the strength of the human spirit. I am deeply grateful for the trust and openness of the veterans I have served, and I am honored to have been a part of their journeys.

As I reflect on the path ahead, I am filled with hope and determination. The future of VA Chaplaincy holds great promise, and I am committed to continuing my work with integrity, compassion, and a deep sense of purpose. Together, we will continue to provide the spiritual care and support that our veterans need, honoring their service and ensuring their well-being for years to come.

Thank you for allowing me to share my journey and for supporting the important work of VA Chaplains. It is a privilege to serve those who have served, and I am humbled by the opportunity to make a difference in their lives.

# APPENDIX

---

## RESOURCES FOR VETERANS

## RESOURCES FOR SPIRITUAL SUPPORT

This appendix provides a comprehensive list of resources for veterans seeking spiritual support. These resources include contact information for VA Chaplain services, support groups, and various religious organizations. Whether you are looking for one-on-one counseling, community support, or specific religious services, the following resources can help you find the spiritual care and guidance you need.

# VA Chaplain Services

## *VA National Chaplain Center*

The National Chaplain Center provides spiritual care services to veterans and their families across the United States. They offer a range of services including counseling, worship services, and support groups.

- **Website:** VA National Chaplain Center
- **Phone:** 1-800-827-1000
- **Address:** 810 Vermont Avenue, NW, Washington, DC 20420

## Local VA Chaplain Services

Each VA Medical Center has chaplain services available to veterans. Contact your local VA Medical Center to connect with a chaplain.

- **Find a VA Medical Center:** VA Facility Locator

# Support Groups

## Veterans Crisis Line

The Veterans Crisis Line provides confidential support for veterans in crisis. They offer immediate assistance and can connect veterans with local resources, including support groups.

- **Website:** Veterans Crisis Line
- **Phone:** 1-800-273-8255 (Press 1)
- **Text:** 838255
- **Chat:** Online Chat

## PTSD Support Groups

Support groups for veterans dealing with PTSD are available at many VA Medical Centers and through various veteran service organizations.

- **Website:** <u>VA PTSD Support</u>
- **Phone:** Contact your local VA Medical Center

## *Grief Support Groups*

Grief support groups provide a space for veterans and their families to share their experiences and find comfort after a loss.

- **Website:** <u>VA Bereavement Support</u>
- **Phone:** Contact your local VA Medical Center

# Religious Organizations

## *American Legion*

The American Legion offers various spiritual support services, including chaplain programs and community support.

- **Website:** <u>American Legion</u>
- **Phone:** 1-800-433-3318

## *Veterans of Foreign Wars (VFW)*

VFW provides spiritual support through its chaplain programs and local posts.

- **Website:** <u>VFW</u>
- **Phone:** 1-833-VFW-VETS (1-833-839-8387)

## *Military Chaplains Association*

The Military Chaplains Association offers resources and support for veterans seeking spiritual care.

- **Website:** Military Chaplains Association
- **Phone:** 1-703-533-5890

# Religious Organizations by Faith

### Christian Resources

National Association of Catholic Chaplains

- **Website:** NACC
- **Phone:** 1-414-483-4898

Lutheran Church - Missouri Synod (LCMS) Ministry to the Armed Forces

- **Website:** LCMS Armed Forces
- **Phone:** 1-888-843-5267

Episcopal Church Office of the Bishop Suffragan for the Armed Forces and Federal Ministries

- **Website:** Episcopal Armed Forces
- **Phone:** 1-800-334-7626

### Jewish Resources

Jewish War Veterans of the USA

- **Website:** JWV
- **Phone:** 1-202-265-6280

Union for Reform Judaism Military Chaplaincy Program

- **Website:** URJ Military Chaplaincy
- **Phone:** 1-212-650-4000

## Muslim Resources

Islamic Society of North America (ISNA) Chaplaincy Services

- **Website:** ISNA Chaplaincy
- **Phone:** 1-317-839-8157

American Muslim Armed Forces and Veterans Affairs Council

- **Website:** AMAFVAC
- **Phone:** 1-703-642-0037

## Buddhist Resources

Buddhist Churches of America

- **Website:** BCA
- **Phone:** 1-415-776-5600

Soka Gakkai International - USA (SGI-USA)

- **Website:** SGI-USA
- **Phone:** 1-310-288-1800

## Hindu Resources

Hindu American Foundation

- **Website:** HAF

- **Phone:** 1-202-223-8222

Vedic Foundation

- **Website:** Vedic Foundation
- **Phone:** Contact through the website

# Conclusion

The resources listed in this appendix provide a starting point for veterans seeking spiritual support. Whether through VA Chaplain services, support groups, or religious organizations, veterans can find the guidance and community they need to navigate their spiritual journeys. These resources are dedicated to honoring the diverse beliefs and experiences of veterans, ensuring that they receive the compassionate and respectful care they deserve.

# FURTHER READING

For those interested in deepening their understanding of veterans' affairs, chaplaincy, and pastoral care, the following books and resources offer valuable insights and information. These recommendations cover a range of topics, including spiritual care, mental health, ethical considerations, and the unique challenges faced by veterans.

## Books on Veterans' Affairs

*1.* The Things They Cannot Say: Stories Soldiers Won't Tell You About What They've Seen, Done or Failed to Do in War *by Kevin Sites*

This book provides firsthand accounts from soldiers, offering a deep and personal look into the experiences and psychological impacts of war.

*2.* Odysseus in America: Combat Trauma and the Trials of Homecoming *by Jonathan Shay*

Jonathan Shay, a psychiatrist specializing in PTSD, explores the psychological effects of combat and the challenges veterans face when returning to civilian life.

*3.* Once a Warrior Always a Warrior: Navigating the Transition from Combat to Home--Including Combat Stress, PTSD, and mTBI *by Charles W. Hoge*

A comprehensive guide to understanding and navigating the transition from combat to civilian life, addressing mental health issues such as PTSD and traumatic brain injury.

# Books on Chaplaincy and Pastoral Care

*1.* The Work of the Chaplain *by Naomi K. Paget and Janet R. McCormack*

This book provides an overview of the diverse roles and responsibilities of chaplains in various settings, including healthcare, military, and institutional chaplaincy.

*2.* Pastoral Care: An Essential Guide *by John Patton*

A practical guide to providing pastoral care, covering essential skills, ethical considerations, and the importance of self-care for caregivers.

*3.* Military Ministry: A Guide for Chaplains *by Dick Stenbakken*

An insightful resource specifically for military chaplains, offering practical advice on providing spiritual support to service members and their families.

# Books on Spiritual and Emotional Healing

*1.* The Wounded Healer: Ministry in Contemporary Society *by Henri J.M. Nouwen*

Henri Nouwen explores the concept of healing through ministry, emphasizing the importance of compassion and vulnerability in providing spiritual care.

*2.* Soul Repair: Recovering from Moral Injury after War *by Rita Nakashima Brock and Gabriella Lettini*

This book addresses the concept of moral injury and offers pathways to healing for veterans grappling with the moral and ethical challenges of their service.

*3.* Healing the Wounds of War: A Spiritual Guide *by Michael L. McGee*

A spiritual guide for veterans seeking healing and reconciliation, offering practical exercises and reflections to support their journey.

# Books on Ethical Considerations in Chaplaincy

*1.* Ethics in the Sanctuary: Examining the Practices of Organized Religion *by Margaret A. Farley*

A thorough examination of ethical issues in religious practice, offering valuable insights for chaplains navigating complex ethical dilemmas.

*2.* Professional Spiritual and Pastoral Care: A Practical Clergy and Chaplain's Handbook *by Rabbi Stephen B. Roberts*

This comprehensive handbook covers ethical considerations, best practices, and practical advice for chaplains and clergy providing spiritual care.

*3.* Caring for Souls: Counseling Under the Authority of Scripture *by Harry E. Shields and Gary J. Bredfeldt*

An exploration of the ethical and theological foundations of pastoral care, emphasizing the importance of integrity and ethical practice.

# Academic Journals and Articles

*1.* Journal of Pastoral Care & Counseling (JPCC)

An academic journal offering research articles, case studies, and practical insights related to pastoral care and counseling.

*2.* Military Medicine

A journal that includes articles on the mental health and well-being of military personnel and veterans, including the role of chaplaincy in their care.

## *3.* Journal of Religion and Health

This journal explores the intersection of religion, spirituality, and health, providing valuable research and perspectives for chaplains and spiritual caregivers.

# Online Resources

## *1.* Veterans Affairs Chaplaincy

The official VA Chaplaincy website offers resources, news, and information about the services provided by VA Chaplains.

- **Website:** VA Chaplaincy

## *2.* National Center for PTSD

The National Center for PTSD provides resources and research on PTSD, including tools and information for veterans and their caregivers.

- **Website:** National Center for PTSD

## *3.* Association of Professional Chaplains (APC)

The APC offers resources, certification information, and continuing education for professional chaplains.

- **Website:** APC

# Conclusion

The resources listed above provide a wealth of information for those interested in veterans' affairs, chaplaincy, and pastoral care. Whether you are a chaplain, a caregiver, or someone seeking to understand the unique challenges faced by veterans, these books and resources offer valuable insights and guidance. By continuing to educate ourselves and engage with these topics, we can better support the spiritual and emotional well-being of veterans and their families.

# ACKNOWLEDGEMENTS

This book would not have been possible without the support, contributions, and encouragement of many individuals who have dedicated their lives to serving veterans and providing spiritual care.

First and foremost, I want to express my deepest gratitude to the veterans who shared their stories and experiences with me. Your courage, resilience, and openness have been a source of inspiration and have profoundly shaped this work. Your willingness to share your journeys has provided invaluable insights into the challenges and triumphs of life after service.

I extend my heartfelt thanks to my fellow VA Chaplains. Your dedication, compassion, and unwavering commitment to serving veterans are truly remarkable. I have been privileged to work alongside many of you, learning from your experiences and witnessing the profound impact of your ministry. Special thanks to Chaplains Sarah, David, Maria, and James, whose stories and examples have enriched this book.

To my colleagues in the field of chaplaincy and pastoral care, thank you for your support, collaboration, and shared wisdom. Your contributions to the field have been invaluable, and I am grateful for the many discussions, workshops, and conferences that have deepened my understanding and practice. A special acknowledgment goes to the National Association of Veterans Affairs Chaplains and the Association of Professional Chaplains for their continued advocacy and support of chaplaincy as a profession.

I also want to acknowledge the support and guidance of my mentors and supervisors, whose advice and encouragement have been instrumental throughout my journey. Your insights and feedback have been invaluable in shaping this book and my approach to spiritual care.

To the families of veterans, thank you for your strength and resilience. Your love and support are essential to the well-being of our veterans, and your experiences have provided important perspectives that have informed this work.

A special thank you to the editorial and publishing team who helped bring this book to life. Your expertise, patience, and dedication have been crucial in transforming this manuscript into a finished book.

Finally, I am profoundly grateful to my own family and friends for their unwavering support and understanding. Your encouragement has sustained me through the challenges of writing this book, and your belief in the importance of this work has been a constant source of motivation.

This book is dedicated to all who serve and have served, and to those who support them. May it honor your sacrifices and contribute to the ongoing mission of providing compassionate and inclusive spiritual care to all veterans.

www.ingramcontent.com/pod-product-compliance
Lightning Source LLC
Chambersburg PA
CBHW071940150726
47999CB00001B/274